More advance praise for Shirt of Flame: The Secret Gay Art of War

by Ko Imani

"Ko Imani's work has a lot of implications for 'next steps' of our human development, a way though our present chaos into a possible whole, liberated, celebration of life on Earth as the ultimate extended family."

~Louis Alemayehu, Community Leader, Minneapolis, MN

"Taking old strategies of nonviolent social change touted by Gandhi and King, Ko Imani reshapes them into an exciting new strategy for Gay, Lesbian, Bisexual, Transgender and Queer liberation. By first focusing our efforts on the inside to become the change we wish to see in the world, Ko lays the groundwork for effective social action. By donning a 'Shirt of Flame,' GLBT people learn the inward spiritual principles and outward practical actions that will lead to not only a civil rights revolution, but also to a revolution of the human heart."

~Candace Chellew, Founder and Editor of
Whosoever: An Online Magazine for GLBT Christians (Whosoever.org)

"If you think gay culture has passed its peak, consider that maybe we've barely scratched the surface. Ko Imani reveals how doing for others may be the best thing we can do for ourselves, to emerge from isolation and fear into loving connectedness. The author uses a global scope of myth, tradition and history to persuade us it's time to wake up and get involved, and to really begin sharing our special gifts as gay people."

~ Bruce P. Grether, author of *Mindful Masturbation:*
Transforming Male Self-Pleasuring into a Spiritual Practice

"Ko Imani's Shirt of Flame is a fine and passionate manifesto. A call to loving arms, the book is a warm reinterpretation of E Pluribus Unum, written as a well-reasoned, heartfelt bridge to a new tradition of morality that is inclusive and profound."

~ Bo Young, Editor of *White Crane Journal*

"To paraphrase John Stuart Mill, 'Were there but a few hearts and intellects like Ko Imani's, this earth would already become the hoped-for heaven.'"

~Jim Toy, Co-Founder of the First Queer Staff Office
at a U.S. Institution of Higher Learning (University of Michigan, 1971)

There's more than one way to flame...

SHIRT OF FLAME
THE SECRET GAY ART OF WAR

by
KO IMANI

"Beauty, no doubt, does not make revolutions.

But a day will come when

revolutions will have need of beauty."

—Albert Camus, *The Rebel*

PUBLISHED BY GOKO MEDIA
P.O. Box 970688
Ypsilanti, MI 48197-0688

GOKO MEDIA, FIRST EDITION, JUNE 2003

Designed by Ko Imani with Pamela Waxman.

Printed in the United States of America

ISBN 0-9741265-0-0

FOR MICHAEL GIBSON-FAITH

my best friend, lover, hero, inspiration and partner.
Shirt of Flame and I would not exist without him.

ACKNOWLEDGMENTS

Thanks first of all to those who brought me into the world, my endlessly supportive mother, Gwen, and my devoted father, Ken, who unfortunately never got to read *Shirt of Flame* and is missed terribly. Thanks also to my brother and sister-in-law, Ken and Kristin, whose affirmation creates a home for Mike and me wherever they are.

Bill Carpenter and Jim Toy have been my biggest boosters and benefactors, even financially supporting the writing of *Shirt of Flame*. Powerful women who encouraged me to share this work with the world include: Julia Mossbridge, the author of *Unfolding* who went out of her way to help someone she's still never met; Kara Speltz, one of the Lesbian saints, Candace Chellew, the editor of Whosoever.org who encouraged me to continue writing my FIRE IN THE LAKE column; and Ann Pacth, Natalie Holbrook and Hillary Stevenson, who were kind enough to proofread the text. Thanks also to Richard Haughton, whose beautiful artwork graces the cover.

And, of course, without my partner's inspiration, support, and understanding, this project would never have happened. Mike and our puppies, Leelu and P'u, bring new joy and blessings into my life every day. I am eternally grateful to them and to the universe that brought us together.

The dove descending breaks the air

With flame of incandescent terror

Of which the tongues declare

The one discharge from sin and error.

The only hope, or else despair

    Lies in the choice of pyre or pyre—

    To be redeemed from fire by fire.

    Who then devised the torment?

Love is the unfamiliar Name

Behind the hands that wove

The intolerable shirt of flame

Which human power cannot remove.

    We only live, only suspire

    Consumed by either fire or fire.

    from *Little Gidding* by T.S. Eliot

1
THE SCHOOL OF FIVE WEAPONS

Once upon a time, thousands of years ago, somewhere in Asia, a handsome young prince had just finished his military studies with a famous teacher. He received the title "Prince Five-weapons" as a symbol of his distinction, and accepted the bow and arrows, sword, spear, and club his teacher gave him. The young prince bowed, and, armed with his knowledge and new weapons, struck out onto the road leading to the city of his parents, the queen and king. On the way he came to the edge of a forest. The villagers that lived nearby warned him, "Beautiful prince, do not enter this forest! An ogre named Sticky-hair, who kills every man he sees, lives here."

But the prince was confident and he fearlessly entered the forest despite their warning. When he reached the heart of it, the ogre showed himself. The ogre was gruesome—as tall as a palm tree with a head as big as a house with a bell-shaped roof, yellow eyes as big as bowls, and two tusks like a bull elephant; he had the beak of a hawk; his body was covered with a tangle of moist gray hair, and his hands and feet were stained dark green. "Where are you going in such a hurry? Won't you stay for dinner, dinner?" the ogre demanded in a hungry growl.

Prince Five-weapons answered without fear, for he had great confidence in the military skills that he had learned. "Ogre," he said, "You should be careful about attacking me, for I will shoot you dead with an arrow steeped in poison!" As the ogre lumbered toward him, the young prince fitted to his bow an arrow coated with deadly poison and let fly. It stuck harmlessly right in the ogre's hair. Then he shot fifty arrows, one after another. All stuck right to the ogre's hair without piercing the fearsome beast. The ogre grinned, shook like a great dog, each one of those arrows falling right at his feet, and continued toward the young prince.

Prince Five-weapons gave the ogre a second warning, and swinging his sword, delivered his most powerful stroke, which could have felled a bodhi tree. The sword stuck right to the ogre's hair. Then the prince tried to impale him with the spear. That also stuck right to his impenetrable tangle of hair. Then the prince smote the ogre with his heavy club. That also stuck right to the monster's hair.

When the prince saw that the club had stuck, he said: "Ogre, you have never heard of me before. I am Prince Five-weapons! But when I entered this forest you've infested, I took no account of bows and such weapons; for a weapon is only an extension of a warrior. Now I am going to beat you and pound you into powder and dust!" With a yell he struck the ogre with his right hand. His hand stuck right to the ogre's hair. He struck him with his left hand. That also stuck. He struck him with his right foot. That also stuck. He struck him with his left foot. That also stuck. He slammed his bare chest into the sticky ogre's body. The still-confident prince shouted, "I will beat you with my head and strike you down!" He butted the ogre with his head, which also stuck right to the ogre's hair.

Prince Five-weapons was stuck fast to the ogre's body in six places! But for all that, he was unafraid, undaunted. The ogre, surprised, thought: "This is some lion of a man and no ordinary human! He's to be made an ogre's dinner, but he doesn't seem afraid! Most people tremble or quake in my presence! In all the time I have lived in this forest, I have never seen a human to match him! Why is he unafraid?" Curious, he asked aloud, "Youth, why are you not afraid? I am going to eat you. Why are you not terrified with the fear of death?"

"Why should I be afraid, Sticky-hair? In one life, one death is to be expected. Besides, I have one weapon left—there is a thunderbolt in my belly. If you eat me, you will not be able to digest that secret weapon. It will tear your insides into shreds and tatters and will kill you. If you eat me, we'll both perish. That's why I'm not afraid!"

"What this youth says is true!" thought the ogre, terrified with the fear of death. "My stomach would not be able to digest the thunderbolt of this lion of a man. I don't want to die!" And he let Prince Five-weapons go. The prince sat the rest of the day with the ogre and instructed him in great spiritual truths. The teaching was so obvious and profound that the ogre was transformed into a kind and helpful friend to the villagers living near the forest, who came to trust him to care for their children and defend the village. The young prince continued whistling through the forest, and returned safely home.

Most things begin violently, like matter exploding into being at the beginning of time. Even our lives begin violently, each of us thrust suddenly, unexpectedly, into the glaring and chill world. From birth on, we are bound with a thousand million cultural conventions which we are taught are natural and necessary; we're given a billion expectations and requirements to meet, most inherently violent to our essential nature, queer or not. We are trained to meet aggression with aggression, hate with hate, and violence with violence. By the time we are capable of changing such behaviors, many of us are tamed entirely, conditioned to regard the cold world as if it were Miami.

For too long, many Lesbian, Gay, Bisexual and Transgender (LGBT or queer) people have allowed others to dictate not only what their concerns are but also how those concerns can best be redressed. A lot of us have been following the 'party line' when it comes to LGBT issues instead of deeply considering our own passions and developing our own informed opinions. Moreover, we often alienate those who rock the boat by suggesting that perhaps there could be a more helpful approach to cultural transformation and the enumeration of LGBT rights and recognition. Even in our queer communities we meet both critique and leadership with mistrust, as if our activism cannot withstand scrutiny. The joke "I thought they gave up cannibalism"—"No, but now they only eat their leaders," hits close to home.

Sometimes it seems that there is no plum or satsuma—not even the fruit of freedom—fragrant, moist and sweet enough to tempt same-gender-loving and Transgender people out of the cage of our conventional approaches to creating change, though the door is open—and has always been open, if desperately defended. Avenues to transform society are available to us that would make the ultimate victory of our movement for equal rights, respect and recognition more likely, but our queer communities are like the legendary ostriches that, even when they are released, will stick their heads in sand rather than venture from cages—even when the door stands open, they stay.

Like Prince Five-weapons, we have used every one of the weapons at our disposal to try to defeat our enemies and win our freedom—we have rallied, railed and wailed, we have marched and voted and debated and organized and lobbied—only to have each small advance lodge uselessly in the status quo's "sticky hair." We have used every weapon in our arsenal and now, dangling from the ogre, we are left with only our thunderbolt untried.

The nature of our battle is such that we may choose to continue our fight with the conventional weapons we know, and we are likely to succeed within a century or two. At the same time, I believe that the 'thunderbolt in our belly' is the only weapon pulsing with enough alchemical power to achieve true victory in the next ten years.

True victory, as Prince Five-weapon's myth demonstrates, is the cessation of hostility as well as the co-creation of new harmony and the transformation of the enemy into benevolent spirit. More than Prince Five-weapon's simple cleverness, that divine thunderbolt is the Weapon of Knowledge, the Power of Love, and the Realization of Self—eternally free, sufficient, immanent. We just have to pry our thunderbolts free and allow them to do their work, but if that is our choice, we have to do it *now*.

We feel the claustrophobic gathering of the political sky around us Bi-attractional, Transgender and same-gender-loving people, like the giant, repressive hand of convention clutching at heaven's cloth. All the attention on LGBT people and issues, positive as well as negative, is a direct consequence of our increased visibility and daring, but we're out of time. This storm is going to break, and soon. We must create change now or not in our lifetimes. If each LGBT person does not learn to rise and stride forward, steadily and relentlessly, if we cannot begin to dance our lives with grace, if we refuse to join hands with other queer people and our allies before the rain comes, we will all be meeting avalanches.

The clock sped through our collective adolescence as queer people. We find ourselves, suddenly and largely unprepared, on the brink of our maturity just as the forces and principalities arrayed against us move to abort us. From city council chambers, school board meetings, pulpits and legislatures, anti-queers are demanding our withdrawal—sometimes in the name of patriotism or public safety, and most often in the name of religion—and if they succeed, the legacy of our stillborn movement would be an end, a hopelessness, a quietude—a homeostatic silence into which hatred and fear could swell grossly and unopposed.

For any LGBT people or Allies to remain silent and suffering, unfulfilled, in this time of tribulation is simply suicide by default. Every life deserves more than to remain undeclared, unsupported and shrouded in fear, and every queer alive today has an immediate destiny to fulfill. This "secret gay art of war" uncovers that destiny and spells out the way to true victory.

Like heroines and heroes in a fairy tale, LGBT people are at that point in the quest where all chasms have been crossed, all chimera dispatched, all riddles answered. We have emerged from a cavern onto the mountaintop, where we're faced with the choice between two blazing weapons, a fiery sword or a Shirt of Flame—equally forged of power and pain, but only one of which will win the battle to save kingdom and soul.

We have reached a critical juncture. The decision we make now between fiery sword and shirt of flame will define the existence and pronounce the fate of all LGBT people, born and unborn, for decades to come. To create positive, genuine, lasting change in culture and policy we just have to take up the correct weapon: the thunderbolt—the Shirt of Flame.

Most things begin violently, but then there is always a choice. We cannot choose whether or not we enter the world underwater, in a mansion or in the projects, just as we cannot control the behaviors of peers, caregivers and strangers who train us in the ways of the world. Like clay that wakes up on the potter's wheel, we cannot help our placement nor so much our shape, but, once we are awake, we can each control what is taken into the vessel of our being and, entirely and most importantly, what comes out.

We LGBT people and our allies cannot help the preponderance of error an ignorant and fearful society put into the fashioning of our individual vessels on that tilting potter's wheel. For most of us, the defining process of nurturing was like riding one of the broken machines of creation, wheel spinning vengefully, thoughtlessly deforming us and shrinking us from our natural potential. Now, we can't help shrieking on the wheel as we painfully grow beyond the limitations of ingrained mental models about sexuality and gender. Our feelings in response to unloving, untrue and violent rhetoric and behavior—our indignant anger and our hurt—are all natural and appropriate.

At the same time, we are on the mountaintop. We are choosing between those blazing weapons, fiery sword or shirt of flame. At every moment of our battle for integrity and actual equality, we have our choice of *response* to violence and ignorance. We choose to either wield a sword forged of Fear or wear a garment grown in Love. We choose between conflict and cultivation. If we want to end oppression, we will all have to make the most helpful choice, individually and collectively. Will we choose destruction or growth? Disease or wholeness? Rot or transformation? Lies or truth? Stupefaction or revelation? A weapon of Fear or one of Love?

In all the amazing expanse of our universe, there are only these two fundamental ways to respond to any situation: with Love or with Fear. Think back through your day for a moment in those terms—every action you took today began as a source thought of alarm or attraction. For example, for different people exercising may result from love (i.e. "taking care of my body because I love myself") or from fear of stigma, illness or loneliness. In every moment, you chose, actively or by default, to embody either Fear or Love. The good news is that whichever you chose a moment ago, now you can choose again.

The tendency is to think that you made your choice long ago, with one careless act or a single gentleness. Really, though, the initiation never ends; every moment, each individual is on that mythical mountaintop deciding between Fear and Love. Every moment, each of us has the option to change her or his mind.

We notice what we notice because of who we are. We create ourselves by what we choose to notice. Once this work of self-authorship has begun, we inhabit the world we've created. We self-seal. We don't notice anything except those things that confirm what we already think about who we already are...When we succeed in moving outside our normal processes of self-reference and can look upon ourselves with self-awareness, then we have a chance at changing. We break the seal. We notice something new.

~ Margaret Wheatley

In our battle, choosing the weapon of Love is the first step of a new journey that offers not only ultimate victory but the achievement of our personal and communal full, abundant, and joyful existence. Fear's blade offers only an ending, a trembling and a death.

Neither path is easy. They are twin fires. Making the choice between Love and Fear is to be "Consumed by either fire or fire," as poet T.S. Eliot offers in "Little Gidding." Choosing the path of inspiration and Love leads through a fire all its own, as Love brings up everything unlike itself. No sooner do we declare what we want to have, be and do than everything we don't want shows up at our door! As Marianne Williamson puts it in *Enchanted Love*, "Any time there is a chance for deep love, there is standing in front of that love a wall of fire. That fire might take the form of something burning within you—an inner condition—or it might take the form of an outer circumstance. But there is never love without fire...the presence of that fire does not say, 'Go away'...the presence of that fire says, 'Here, if you are strong enough to take it, is love.'" Choosing Love does not mean we will not be tested and derided, but we can pass through any tempering fire if we only hold to Love. That you undertake this journey at all, even just reading and trying to apply *Shirt of Flame* to your own life, proves your mythic courage.

However, we, the heroines and heroes of our Promethean story, seem to have fallen into the trickster's trap of choosing—like leaving a decision up to committee. We stand with flaming weapon in either hand, weighing our options, swinging first the one, then testing the other. We silently debate which might be the better way to claim our equal rights and recognition, forgetting to actually take one down from the mountain to fight the battle and being burned by both in the meantime!

At least Prometheus climbed Olympus on purpose; he went specifically to steal secret fire. Lesbian, Gay, Bisexual and Transgender 'Olympians,' on the other hand, stumbled onto the mountaintop through an evolutionary process. We didn't ask to be special. Most of us had no ambition to change the world; we just wanted to live happy, abundant and worry-free lives. Even so, make no mistake—like Prometheus', our choices will change everything.

Each of us stands on the mountain alone; you cannot choose between Fear and Love for anyone but yourself. However, it is just as accurate to say that all LGBT people are assembled there at once, since we are not only individuals but a community. Each of us acts not only in isolation but also as part of a social justice movement (whether we're calling Senators and protesting in the streets or not). Keep this in mind, because this dichotomy of alone and together will come up again and again as you read *Shirt of Flame*.

Although we do not doubt that, as anthropologist Margaret Mead said, "a small group of committed citizens can change the world," we must also acknowledge that the queer rights movement as we have known it has floundered largely because of the absence of a mass grass-roots commitment to a specific and effective purpose and methodology. Large state and national LGBT organizations have almost uniformly attempted to create societal change by focusing outward; they have spent most of their time trying to force change on straight people.

In some ways, of course, this is very helpful. Straight people certainly will have to make adjustments in thought, deed and law. At the same time, that cannot be the whole story. LGBT people have changes to make, too, and the positive impact on straight society when we do will outshine all the rest of our efforts. Hopefully *Shirt of Flame* will be of help to you when you make the decision to transform, when you choose to, as Mohandas Gandhi put it, "become the change you wish to see in the world."

As LGBT individuals and as a queer community, the time has come to make a bold and decisive commitment to the most congruent and effective means to create change that we can muster given our current knowledge. We must choose wisely, for only one option nourishes life. Our enemies have already made their choice—the sword of Fear, falsity and dissolution. We must choose growth, wholeness, transcendence, truth, revelation, cultivation and Love!

However, we must remember that Love is not a hoe, not a hammer. Love is not a pen, saw, mask, nor ship to sail across our conflict laying on a daybed eating grapes. Love is not even a weapon. Love may not be wielded and then yielded when the war is won. This Love is the "thunderbolt within," a power which cannot be displaced nor lulled back to sleep once awakened. To choose the instrument of Love is to don the intolerable shirt of flame: to put on the garment, a second and shimmering skin, the very being, of Love. Each of us must *become* Love, in chosen, earthy, and real Incarnation, by choosing to respond to every situation with it.

To become an Incarnation is not to lose one's self. The process and ethics upon which *Shirt of Flame* is based do no harm to individuality or free will. This articulation of a 21st Century queer activism does not require that we all think in exactly the same way, agree as to what our most important issues are, or undertake exactly the same projects to transform culture and society. We will not dissolve into a homogeneous movement but unite into an unbreakable web of snowflakes and sunlight, distinct and glorious.

To weave that web we must determine the strongest connectors between us, including a Love-centered moral basis for action upon which we can all agree. We cannot continuously choose the weapon of Love if we only take action because we feel threatened, maligned and discriminated against!

For most of human history, morality has been defined by large groups of people engaged in one or another religion. However, in the 21st Century we blink and breathe in an age of pluralism. Most people acknowledge that their personal freedom to choose their spiritual journey is threatened when other people are denied the pursuit of other religions, and yet there are so many different religions, with so many moralities, that our society lacks a comprehensive moral rudder. As in life, we can determine which way to go by where our obstacles lie. In this case, "there are too many opinions to be able to set a standard" points to the answer: we must find a moral standard outside of the divisions.

This diverse new millennium requires a morality as powerful as it is comprehensive, fresh and compassionate. We require an ethic that is not rooted in any single church's doctrine or tradition but instead is able to include and transcend the incredible array of human faith traditions and belief systems. To be practical, this Universal Ethical Standard (UES) must also set reasonable limits on what is permissible in a modern and diverse society based on what seems to be the most basic right of living beings: the right of every individual to take action in order to pursue genuine happiness or to avoid suffering.

So, the Universal Ethical Standard defines an acceptable (ethical) act as *any action taken in the pursuit of happiness or in the avoidance of suffering, and which does not infringe upon the happiness of another.* Significantly, the UES is based on our sameness as living beings, not on our differences. Unlike old models, the UES involves a bringing together instead of a dividing. This reflects a truth we've learned from the great spiritual teachers as well as from our own experience: *Fear divides and Love joins.*

Fear is the energy which contracts, closes down, draws in, runs, hides, hoards, harms. Love is the energy which expands, opens up, sends out, stays, reveals, shares, heals. Fear wraps our bodies in clothing, love allows us to stand naked. Fear clings to and clutches all that we have, love gives all that we have away. Fear holds close, love holds dear. Fear grasps, love lets go. Fear rankles, love soothes. Fear attacks, love amends.

~ Neale Donald Walsch

With the Universal Ethical Standard, we claim the freedom imagined by our ancestors: a global society in which all people—regardless of religion, race, sex, gender expression, creed, sexual orientation, political affiliation, and every other separating label between people—are welcomed with equal opportunity for joy in living and peace in dying. Dr. Martin Luther King, Jr. called this vision the "Beloved Community." The King Center explains:

> "Dr. King's Beloved Community is a global vision, in which all people can share in the wealth of the earth. In the Beloved Community, poverty, hunger and homelessness will not be tolerated because international standards of human decency will not allow it. Racism and all forms of discrimination, bigotry and prejudice will be replaced by an all-inclusive spirit of sisterhood and brotherhood. In the Beloved Community, international disputes will be resolved by peaceful conflict-resolution and reconciliation of adversaries, instead of military power. Love and trust will triumph over fear and hatred. Peace with justice will prevail over war and military conflict."

What is a "Beloved Community?"

1. A Just community, where justice, food, shelter, education, employment, health and hope are fairly distributed and where all people participate in government;

2. A Beautiful community, where art, architecture and landscape spark the imagination and move the Spirit;

3. A Creative community, where open-mindedness and experimentation mobilize the full potential of its human resources and allow a fast response to change;

4. An Ecological community, which minimizes its ecological impact, where landscape and built form are balanced and where buildings and infrastructures are safe and resource-efficient;

5. A community of Easy Contact and Mobility, where information is exchanged both face-to-face and electronically;

6. A Compact and Polycentric community, which protects the countryside, focuses and integrates communities within neighborhoods and maximizes proximity; and,

7. A Diverse community, where a broad range of overlapping cultures and activities creates animation, inspiration and fosters a vital public life.

One may (and some probably will) argue that to impress an ethical template like the Universal Ethical Standard on our entire society might bring us to the edge of chaos, or turn the Capital to salt, as our society's prejudicial, patriarchal, heterosexist traditions are gradually transformed by our compassionate fulfillment of a dream of freedom. The point is, of course, that in this case there is a distinct choice: either we choose to engage and fulfill our society's vision of justice, respect and freedom, or we choose to put the lie to innumerable years of inspired and eloquent evolution. Not coincidentally, the choice our nation faces is also the choice for us as LGBT people: Do we claim our lives and loves or relinquish the entire possibility of truly *being* in this life? Do we do what we know is best for us or continue to wallow, struggle and self-destruct?

Although occasionally a government will jump ahead of its citizenry—the United States ending racial segregation, for example—governments usually change as a *result* of popular transformation. If a critical mass of citizens changes their thinking, their representative government—if it is truly representative—will necessarily reflect that change. To achieve lasting victory, in addition to passing laws protecting our rights and relationships, LGBT people must open the hearts and minds of straight people.

This reflects the most basic assumption upon which *Shirt of Flame* is based, which is that the *end* is inherent in the *means*. Hate has never displaced hate, and violence cannot end violence. Demanding change without embodying change will never create change. One cannot separate the result from the process of achieving it.

Because the true freedom and creativity of a Beloved Community is the end we desire, a mass paradigm shift toward refined love and deep nonviolence is required to transform straights' prejudice and our government's policies and to make our nation culturally sustainable. 'Refined love and deep nonviolence' must dictate the process of change because the end we desire is loving, decent, affirming and fraternal. As citizens change one by one, nations change collectively. A thirteen-year study by Paul Ray and Sherry Ruth Anderson estimates that *50 million* such "Cultural Creatives" already live in the United States alone, so the genuine possibility for meaningful change already exists.

Shirt of Flame: The Secret Gay Art of War is a mosaic explanation of motivations and techniques for queer people's conscious self-transformation and for a purely constructive 21st Century LGBT activism. The combination of our personal evolutions and our new activism will arrange the ground for the ultimate cultural and legal victory of the LGBT rights movement. If we are willing to become the embodiment of and the voice for Love, we LGBT and Ally people can lead our nation and the world on the journey toward compassionate actualization of the Beloved Community.

The book's subtitle, "The Secret Gay Art of War," is a reference to the ancient Chinese manual of military strategy, the *Sun Tzu*, or *The Art of War*, which we will discuss more later. Conflict and confrontation are necessarily implied, but the methods of a 'war' fought with a Shirt of Flame are purely constructive, not destructive.

Once we really "get it" that the end is inherent in the means, we begin to understand the potential violence intrinsic in the "us-versus-them" thinking upon which conflict is usually based, and we shift our thinking toward an "us-*and*-them" model. Like an arm or leg, queers cannot be actually separated from the body of society, however much we may be denied or despised, however great our bitterness toward the rest of the body. We must remember that, as Gandhi said, holding onto a policy of "an eye for an eye" just leaves the whole world blind.

We LGBT people are both inseparably part of and at the same time held at a distance from society, but our very peripheral-ness may be our greatest asset! Those of us who have been marginalized by patriarchal, ageist, racist, classist and heterosexist societies—who already feel separated from its culture of Fear—have an advantage because of our isolation. In the same way that it's said that peacocks make their brilliant feathers by eating thorns, we can use the principles in *Shirt of Flame* to transform the darkness and the distance we are given.

The Shirt of Flame path to victory comes easier to those who already feel different and outside the affection of society because for us, the fundamental fear of being perceived as "different" has already been faced! We know, on a deep and personal level, that we have been marginalized because we are "different" in some ways: because of whom and how we love; because we look different or have not lived as long or have lived longer; because our gender identification or behavior is perceived as deviant and / or unnatural; or simply because we fundamentally disagree with various socially-acceptable paradigms and policies.

Differences are, paradoxically, what human beings most value and most despise. Human beings virtually idolize those who, because of their deviation from social norms, inspire us to live our lives more fully—whether that's Madonna or Mohandas K. Gandhi matters little. Even the most privileged middle-class white heterosexual man can feel as much pull to stand out as to blend in; every individual is unique, and we usually reward people who are able to share their uniqueness with us by offering our attention, care and support. Women and men who glory in their uniqueness may remind of us of our own specialness and inspire us to courage and vulnerability. At the same time, at certain levels of development, the prospect of being perceived as different can be very threatening. After all, every act of violence and war has the same origin: that someone or a group of somebodies is different and *other*, and must be possessed, dominated, altered or destroyed.

When we interact with oppressive society from our anger, fear or pain, we actually affirm *to ourselves* the social identification of us as "outside," "different," or "alienated." Adopting a Shirt of Flame method means that we choose, instead, to affirm our constituent and responsible function as part of the body of society. After we have transformed the thorns society gives us into plumage, our outsider status can empower us. We then have the strength and agility to stand up in the boat to challenge groupthink mentality, to boldly point in a new direction across the waters toward the island of a Beloved Community.

This reversal of traditional "us-versus-them" activist thinking is a challenging and assertive affirmation of the society we wish to co-create. We become 'travelers of speed' at the outside edge of culture, great patriots of the ethical, inclusive and harmonious society to come, instead of activists attempting to dominate society differently. Joseph Campbell insightfully said to Bill Moyers in *The Power of Myth* that, "People have the notion of saving the world by shifting things around, changing the rules, and who's on top, and so forth. No, no! Any world is a valid world if it's alive. The thing to do is to bring life to it, and the only way to do that is to find in your own case where the life is and become alive yourself."

Choosing the Shirt of Flame is a commitment to 'finding where the life is and becoming fully alive yourself.' By exploring and defining yourself and your social contributions in new, wholly constructive ways, you will burn with the contrast between your new empowered consciousness and a society around you slumbering in fear.

Dr. King, for example, a black man in a predominantly white and certainly discriminating popular culture, led the African-American civil rights movement in the name of Love and nonviolence. He lived a life and inspired a movement grounded unconditionally in Love, although his life, filled with constant threats of scorn, death and failure, was hardly comfortable. Because he woke himself and millions of others up with the trumpet of justice, he became a target for all that was not just. Love brings up everything unlike itself. Dr. King felt the fires of a Shirt of Flame.

Almost forty years after his assassination, King, like Gandhi before him, continues to be for us a pillar of fire sent into the darkness to light our way. The LGBT movement must carefully consider the past in order to mindfully prepare for the future. Each of us must, in her or his own being, model the change she or he wishes to see in the world by including and transcending the lessons of history—both in struggle and in strategy.

We have the chance at this point in our social evolution, as queer individuals and as an LGBT community, to claim for ourselves freedom's promise of full, joyful and abundant life. No one else can do it for us; no law and no amount of parading and shouting will get us there. The only tool to end bigotry, to end hatred and violence, to end Fear—the only tool we can use to build the Beloved Community—is Love.

We must become the presence of that alternative.

The time has come for us to wake up from our narcoleptic lives.

It is time for us to choose.

Time to take up the weapon of Love.

Time to strip naked on the mountaintop and don the **Shirt of Flame.**

2

THE CRISIS OF MEANS
THE DARKNESS AND THE DISTANCE

"The ultimate weakness of [using violence to stop] violence is that it is a descending spiral, begetting the very thing it seeks to destroy. Instead of diminishing evil, it multiplies it. Through violence you murder the hater, but you do not murder hate. In fact, violence merely increases hate... Returning violence for violence multiplies violence, adding deeper darkness to a night already devoid of stars. Darkness cannot drive out darkness; only light can do that. Hate cannot drive out hate; only love can do that."

~ Dr. Martin Luther King, Jr.

"The theme of the Grail romance is that the land, the country, the whole territory of concern has been laid waste. It is called a wasteland. And what is the nature of the wasteland? It is a land where everybody is living an inauthentic life, doing as other people do, doing as you're told, with no courage for your own life. That is the wasteland..."

~ Joseph Campbell

Lesbian, Gay, Bisexual, and Transgender people must choose to be guided in our lives and our activism by either Love or Fear. One option points right to inevitable destruction and the other angles left, toward life. Today, society is listing to the right and toward its own demise. We LGBT people must act now to lead the entire culture in the healthier direction—the direction of Love. To be successful, we must resolve why and how an LGBT Shirt of Flame movement should proceed. We must understand the environment in which we act and the factors to be considered in making decisions about our journey. We must articulate ultimate goals, and determine creative and congruous means to those ends.

We are going to do a somewhat unfashionable thing to begin, for to speak of the prevailing madness of modern Western society, its blind, bullish charges and its grievous failings, is to elicit yawns at the tired assertions. Tired meaning old news, tired meaning known. Indeed, despite plug-in scents like affirmative action, welfare, hate crimes legislation, philanthropy and other exercises of rhetoric and field dressing, the heart of a self-destructive and violent society beats always just underneath the floorboards, known but too familiar to wrench a soul's attention. Like muzak or water running, things become invisible to us when they're there all the time.

Let's not talk about a society that is dead or dying but of an ideal gravely endangered. For all its disappointments, modern democratic society is an excellent model because it is based, albeit inchoately, on the democratic and humanistic ideals of equality and respect. American society, for example, is great because it *will* be great if it can fulfill its promise, not because it necessarily is presently. The mammoth potentiality of the United States is an unfocused evolutionary spurt despite its lofty apotheoses, easily perverted to self-serving ends by those of power and influence instead of guided toward the embodiment of its ideals: Equality of Rights and Opportunity; *E Pluribus Unum* or Unity in Diversity; Balance of Individual Liberty and Protection of the Common Good; and Religious Freedom. You don't have to read very many headlines before you realize that perversion of the USA's potential has become commonplace, regardless of the cost in human suffering at home and abroad.

All around, the deaf and encroaching desiccation of modern society is unmistakable. It's expressed in our deteriorating physical environment and violent and competitive culture; in a general cynicism, apathy and hopelessness among our people; in the West's persistent abuse of minorities across the globe; in our veneration of individual ego and corporate health over community; in our obscene hesitance to transform negative social situations by embracing positive solutions at hand; in a self-perpetuating politics of corruption, power and money; and in our dedication to an endless war. A deficient or inauthentic application of the democratic ideals of justice and liberty is the root of all these problems, along with a pervasive disbelief in these self-declared absolutes. That disbelief leads us to unjustified compromise with the less-than ideal, the dissolving, the 'evil.'

Not enough people deeply understand or believe in our fundamental ideals, and therefore the majority's citizen power to force social-actualization is abdicated to others who often believe exclusively in politics, profit and pleasure. There is little faith and much bitterness, impatience and skepticism among people about the possibility that modern democratic societies could fulfill their destiny by establishing the Beloved Community.

By donning Shirts of Flame, Lesbian, Gay, Bisexual and Transgender people are entering into our incarnations of Love in the middle of this stumbling progress, this ravaged landscape of modern society and ideals. Of course, there are and have always been people everywhere with seeing eyes and attendant ears fighting against the spread of these calamitous circumstances; pockets, oases, scattered but all inflamed by the same 'force that through the green fuse drives the flower.' There are so many of these that to attempt examples would inevitably omit many worthy people. Unfortunately, to date, these folk are usually too scattered, their collective energy too diffused, their individual focuses too narrow to force the hand of real, widespread, peaceful, evolutionary change.

Evolution always incorporates and transcends, and this evolutionary principle is the visionary function of Western social systems. Foremost, "We hold these Truths to be self-evident, that all [people] are created equal, that they are endowed by their Creator with certain unalienable Rights, that among these are Life, Liberty, and the Pursuit of Happiness." The Grand Experiment of the United States is to equally include all people and all traditions and belief systems, and then to move beyond those differences to mass prosperity, health and happiness— 'to incorporate and transcend.'

The persistent idea that a conservative minority should determine whether or not the social evolution of the United States, or any country, is acceptable is ridiculous. This incorporation and transcendence of genders, ideologies, cultures, ethnicities, abilities and sexualities is the basis on which such nations are founded—not optional. After all, things are true because they are so *all* the time, not because they are relative, subject to the fluidity of dogma. If Equality of Rights and Opportunities is a first principle of a society, then everyone in that society should be guaranteed equal rights and equal opportunities, no questions asked.

"We are simply seeking to bring into full realization the American dream— a dream yet unfulfilled. A dream of equality of opportunity, of privilege and property widely distributed; a dream of a land where men[sic] no longer argue that the color of a man's skin [or a person's sexual orientation or gender identity] determines the content of his character; the dream of a land where every man will respect the dignity and worth of human personality—this is the dream. When it is realized, the jangling discords of our nation will be transformed into a beautiful symphony of brotherhood."

~ Martin Luther King, Jr.

The evolutionary principle to include and transcend is woven into the first principles of modern, democratic societies. The opportunities that our social evolution promises is what compels immigrants from across the world to risk all they have to join in the dream. Doesn't every reasonable person wants Religious Freedom, respect for Diversity, Equal Rights and Opportunities and a Balance of Individual Liberty with the Common Good? Constant compromise of our progression toward actualizing those first principles demeans us all, and demands response.

To respond well, we must first overcome our general narcolepsy, a self-protective response to suffering and the naked face of too much reality. We are like slaves on a silicon plantation in wartime, doped with narcotics of distraction and desensitization to ensure our languor, our disinterest. Our society has managed to convince us that decoupage is democracy, that we have neither power nor place to relieve even our own suffering, much less anyone else's. Even the awakening that led to the peace rallies of 2002 and 2003 does not reflect the scale of arousal necessary to effect a change. Tradition, jingoism and the status quo are mighty powers for us to transform.

In this 21st Century, human beings are at once more connected to the world, at least in communication capability, and increasingly distanced from one another, from victory and tragedy, from the truth behind news headlines, the experience, from possibility and from rain. This arrangement does not benefit us, the people; it benefits only those who either profit from our labor or appropriate our divested power.

Most urgently and importantly, we have to wake up and face head-on the causes of our and others' suffering. We cannot eliminate the causes of suffering by addressing their effects, just like a doctor doesn't treat the flu by holding the patient's hair back. We have to become antibodies that can recognize the *roots* of suffering and then unearth them with grace.

So, we come through this wasteland of inured silence, this still land of inaction despite overwhelming evidence of injustice—a wasteland of inauthentic, pathological living and co-created suffering. We come as Bisexual, Transgender, Gay and Lesbian people disenfranchised from the full, abundant and joyful lives to which we are inherently entitled as human beings, and implicitly guaranteed by most Constitutions and Bills of Rights as well as the United Nation's Universal Declaration of Human Rights. Each of us comes ready to claim the fulfillment of her or his positive potential and to force the evolution of human society using the only tool that can make of the wasteland a garden. The weapon of Love. The Shirt of Flame.

THE WILL TO POWER

One reason that the queer rights movement's successes have been few is because our activists used confused and conflicting means to pursue their ends. Everyone may want to be happy and avoid suffering, but much LGBT activism of the latter 20th Century was motivated by desperation, pain and anger. Many heroines and heroes of the infamous uprising at the Stonewall Inn in New York City, usually credited with starting the queer rights movement as we know it today, responded to police brutality with thrown rocks and intentional fires. In the 1980's and early 1990's, the holocaust of gay men stricken with AIDS as well as governments' homophobic silence, ignited hundreds of confrontational direct actions, such as the storming of the Archbishop of Canterbury's pulpit on Easter Sunday.

Queer activism at the end of the 20th Century was often aggressive and seemingly intended to demand attention and intimidate and bully adversaries to retreat. These important activists modeled for all queers the courage to stand up for ourselves without shame, and to dare to make our voices and concerns heard. Their work required great bravery and confidence, and, if they had stayed silent, LGBT people would not enjoy the level of social acceptance that we do today. Silence, as their slogan said, Equals Death.

At the same time, despite the many young and closeted LGBT individuals they inspired and the advances they successfully demanded, the social legacy of this aggressive activism is mixed. Although much of society appreciated queer activists' desire to be heard, valued and protected, a significant portion of the heterosexual population continues to bear attitudinal scars from their experience of gay aggression. As Straightpride.com once posited, "the loudness of gay rights has put many citizens who embrace family values on the defensive." The conclusion seems elementary, but is dismissed by many LGBT activists as "not our problem."

Heterosexuals' symptoms seem to be a combination of homeostasis, a condition of equilibrium that is highly resistant to change, and a form of *'future shock'*, "the shattering stress and disorientation that we induce in individuals by subjecting them to too much change in too short a time." The demands of the modern age require rapid change, beyond many people's capacity to cope, so although queer and other progressive activists pushed for *necessary* and *just* changes, their efforts were an easy scapegoat for a heterosexual, homeostatic public already overloaded with radical, fast-paced change.

It certainly didn't help that LGBT activism of the day frequently took little care for the psychological and emotional well-being of heterosexual people, choosing to focus on shock, demonization and intimidation as its tools of change. The "Queer Nation Manifesto" of 1990 went so far as to say:

> "Straight people will not [eliminate straight privilege] voluntarily and so they must be forced into it. Straights must be frightened into it. Terrorized into it. Fear is the most powerful motivator. No one will give us what we deserve. Rights are not given they are taken, by force if necessary. It is easier to fight when you know who your enemy is. Straight people are your enemy... I hate straights."

Is it any wonder many heterosexuals continue to be both hesitant to publicly support our cause and antagonistic in response to our demands for their support?

Leading American philosopher Ken Wilber points out that our astonishing belief "that acceptance of my group [for example, LGBT people] can be accomplished by aggressively blaming and condemning exactly the group from which I seek the acceptance [i.e. straight people]" is a type of *pathological pluralism*. Given many heterosexuals' negative reactions, this belief doesn't appear to serve us well.

Forty-six percent (46%!) of those participating in a January 2002 survey on Beliefnet.com agreed that they perceived fewer people speaking out against homosexuality not because their beliefs have changed but because "They feel threatened by gay rights groups or by expectations of political correctness." Sixteen percent agreed that people with gay-critical opinions were "being silenced or censored."

BELIEFNET.COM survey (Results pulled 9 JANUARY 2002)

I think the reason fewer people are speaking out against homosexuality is:

They are being silenced or censored—16%

They feel threatened by gay rights groups
or by expectations of political correctness—46%

They have changed their views and/or
sincerely do not want to—23%

It's not true that fewer people are speaking out—15%

Obviously, we do not hope for *more* anti-queer expression, except as an alternative to repressed, invisible prejudice. What is significant about Beliefnet's survey is that so many surveyed felt that heterosexuals' very ability to express themselves is being restricted, limited or threatened.

The popular understanding is that "You can't say that [anti-LGBT remark]" is a safe-space-creating precursor to a culture of heterosexuals who would never say something like that. Still, however efficacious and welcome it makes LGBT people feel to enforce as much politically correct conversation as possible, it seems to be alienating the very people whose hearts and minds we need to open.

At the same time, putting so much effort into demanding that straight people liberate us may be an outright waste. Paulo Freire writes in *Pedagogy of the Oppressed* that:

> "Although the situation of oppression is a dehumanized and dehumanizing totality affecting both the oppressors and those whom they oppress, it is the latter who must, from their stifled humanity, wage for both the struggle for a fuller humanity; the oppressor, who is himself dehumanized because he dehumanizes others, is unable to lead this struggle."

Queer liberation is ultimately LGBT people's responsibility, not heterosexuals', since, as Feire says, they are "unable to lead this struggle." It falls to LGBT people to "wage *for both* the struggle for a fuller humanity." One of the main ideas we have to overcome is the half-truth upon which most queer activism is based. This message, that we get from so many of the public figures and organizations that usually direct the LGBT movement, is: "If queers are to be free from closets, discrimination, violence and harassment, legislators will have to pass laws, ministers will have to adjust their rhetoric, Hollywood will have to put more queer-positive roles in straight movies, school systems will have to teach healthy sexuality and dialogue skills, and communities will have to learn to find unity in diversity."

In short, "Those people over there are going to have to change."

Very convenient, isn't it? Places all the responsibility for transformation on other people—legislators, ministers, filmmakers, educators and nebulous 'communities,' for example—and leaves us absolved of any responsibility at all.

According to this half-truth, the only duty of LGBT people (notice how very perspicacious we are!) is to force those great stumbling sillies to make the changes that they need to make for us to feel safe, happy and welcome. And, if straight people do not change in the ways we'd like in the time frame we'd prefer, it's obvious where the blame lies—"Over there!"

The other half of the truth, often put on the table by anti-LGBT people, is that it's queers who need to change. Usually they mean that we need to change our gender or affectional expression, or that we should stop demanding our "special" rights. The kind of change they demand is wrong, but we LGBT people do have some changing of our own to do.

Put the two half-truths together and we have a whole. The answer is both-and, not either-or. If Bisexual, Transgender, Lesbian and Gay women and men are going to be truly free, everybody's got some growing to do. Legitimation and its social, legal, cultural, and political mainstreaming will only fully arrive after queers liberate ourselves from our habitual ways of creating change as well as from the thoughts and internalized negativity that hold us back. Much of the misunderstandings and harm that result from aggressive LGBT activism are because of our activists' push for legitimation before liberation.

Strictly speaking, queers are *not* responsible for the negative reactions of many heterosexuals to our activism, but at the same time, it's easy to see how queer antagonism and loudly enforced political correctness contribute to their negative attitudes about queer people and issues. Negative attitudes on *both* sides act as a barrier to establishing the Beloved Community. Reinforcing that barrier is an unfortunate byproduct of aggressive queer activism.

OUR MOVING FORWARD HOLDS US BACK

The pursuit of worthy goals (happiness, freedom, security, integrity, etc.) through aggressive means has negative consequences for both LGBT activists who undertake such activism and the heterosexuals toward whom such activism is directed. How human beings act, what we think and what we say effect how we *feel* and create habitual patterns of behavior.

Aggressive thoughts, words or actions compound one's negative and discontent attitude, increasing the likelihood of generally negative and aggressive attitudes and behaviors in the future. Distress caused by negativity even makes one's body less able to fight disease.

We cannot establish the Beloved Community while queer activism is based on aggression and antagonistic thinking. We cannot replace bigotry and prejudice with "an all-inclusive spirit of sisterhood and brotherhood" as long as any queer still says "I hate straights" or any heterosexual genuinely believes her or his way of life is threatened. Love and trust cannot triumph over Fear and hatred while queers and straights attack and demonize one another.

To establish the Beloved Community, we have to let go of our attempts to dominate and give in to our innate drive to connect, to love. As psychoanalyst Carl Jung noted, "Where the will to power is paramount love will be lacking."

Hindsight being 20/20, it's understandable that queers resorted to aggressive activism, not just because of the desperate climate created by heterosexism, homonegativity and epidemic disease, but as an expression of the traditional will to power. Most of us learned while growing up that power was the ability to achieve one's goals or desires by controlling, dominating or manipulating others, or as Napoleon suggested, by hiding one's iron hand in a velvet glove. This traditional will to power is deeply ingrained in Western social structures, from politics to school systems and family dynamics. So, naturally, many of our activists pursued this kind of power.

Power has ethically dubious connotations of domination for most people. Historical knowledge of the actions of the 'power-hungry' of the past, as well as our own formative experiences of being dominated, manipulated or controlled, may make the pursuit or possession of power, at best, uncomfortable, and at worst, despicable.

Despite the fact that an ability to influence the outer world is an essential part of our self-esteem, we may see power as undesirable or inherently corrupted or corrupting because we have only witnessed the traditional will to power. We may feel desperately guilty or ashamed because of what we do to achieve our goals. We may deny our own will to power, repressing awareness of the actions we take to get what we desire from others. In the end, we may simply live in denial of an important part of our existence as human beings of a time and place. This kind of dissociation is psychologically unhealthy. Consciously or unconsciously, as long as we have desires, we have a will to power.

TRUE POWER

Wearing the Shirt of Flame does not mean that we relinquish our will to power. In fact, the Shirt of Flame is a tool we use to achieve power, but power redefined. True Power is the ability to achieve one's goals and desires through self-control, self-knowledge, and (this is the biggie) *through influence with others resulting from communion and trust.*

This Power is the antithesis of traditional power because we do not pursue Power through the domination, manipulation or control of others. Our Power results from healthy relationships with ourselves, other queers, heterosexuals and heterosexual society, and the natural world.

The 14th Dalai Lama tells a story about his childhood in which one of his attendants (and a rather unattractive monk, at that, the young Dalai Lama thought) had befriended a beautiful parrot. The parrot would get very excited whenever this monk approached, or even if he just coughed or spoke nearby.

The young Dalai Lama was very jealous of his attendant's relationship with the bird, and desired to have a similar relationship with the bird. Unfortunately, the parrot did not like the Dalai Lama! He would not let the Dalai Lama stroke him or feed him like the other monk did. The Dalai Lama tried poking the bird with a stick, hoping to get a better reaction. Of course, this only frightened the parrot, which, from then on, would only try to keep as far away from the Dalai Lama as possible! The young Dalai Lama had destroyed whatever scant prospect for friendliness existed between them.

Understandable as it is that we may have made clumsy attempts to achieve our goals and desires, with fortunate and unfortunate consequences for others and ourselves, we must learn to apply the insight that genuine Power is primarily based on communion and trust and cannot be cultivated with any kind of aggression. "Poking the parrot" will never make of the bird a friend.

ATTENTION MUST BE PAID

To successfully develop communion and build trust, we must practice this new will to Power very consciously. We also must develop discipline about the content of and intention behind every exercise of desire we undertake. When we act to achieve a goal or desire, we must act mindfully so that we don't cause harm, especially damage that persists longer than the benefit! This means that our actions must be held to a higher standard, and always be focused on the end goal, the establishment of the Beloved Community, instead of on short-term relief or gain.

Those who only understand power as a result of domination, control and manipulation will try to define us in their terms. They will accuse queers who choose Shirts of Flame of simply being sneaky; they will accuse us of being manipulative and duplicitous. "You're just trying to get underneath and behind people's barriers," they'll say of our efforts to cultivate community. "You don't really care about anyone but yourselves. This drive to establish 'communion and trust' is just a way for you to trick everyone into thinking the way you do without them knowing it."

In *The 48 Laws of Power*, Robert Greene writes that those who profess distaste for traditional power "flaunt their moral qualities, their piety, their exquisite sense of justice...in fact they are often the ones most skillful at indirect manipulation...And they greatly resent any publicizing of the tactics they use every day."

Of course, this is one way of looking through Napoleonic eyes at the nonviolent development of the Power of communion. Such a cynical, jaded and outdated (i.e. traditional) point of view is only helpful in analyzing our Shirt of Flame insomuch as it prepares us to deal with how critics may place very negative judgments on our new, 21st century LGBT activism. This pointed criticism will come from those who have either been repeatedly hurt by exercises of domination, manipulation and control or are most invested in the status quo of traditional power, whether maintaining it or fighting it.

Certainly, our particular will to power exists, as certain as the rotation of the earth. However, because we recognize the suffering that others' traditional domination models already wreak on cultures and people across the world, we relinquish any desire to dominate, manipulate or deceive others into transforming their attitudes about LGBT people and issues.

The goals and desires we wish to achieve are undeniable among friends: to live freely, securely and happily, and with abundance and integrity. This means that each of us must shift her or his focus from what heterosexuals and heterosexist society are withholding to developing constructive relationships with them.

"DOCTOR, DOCTOR, IT HURTS WHEN I DO THIS..."

Many LGBT activists approach their activism the way Rod Tidwell, Cuba Gooding, Jr.'s character in the 1996 film *Jerry Maguire*, approaches football. As Tom Cruise's character, Jerry, puts it, "When you're out there it's all about what you're not getting! Who's not giving you your contract. Who's not giving you your 'kwan.' And that is *not* what inspires people."

Along the same lines, Ram Dass tells Mark Thompson in *Gay Soul*, "If I have a model that society should act a certain way toward me and they don't, I suffer. If I don't have that model, I don't suffer—they act the way they do, and I'm responding like a tree on a river. The tree doesn't have a model for how the river should be."

We actually participate in the creation of our experiences through our reactions to our circumstances. When we deny this truth, it's easy to climb onto a very high horse and out of that perspicacious feeling of superiority and 'victim mind' to wag a finger and say, "Society, you should treat me better!" Of course, then we experience existential suffering because of the lack that we perceive.

We would not *experience* our condition as innately unsatisfactory if we did not cling to the idea that we were 'without.' With external forces, we are complicit in co-creating our psychological suffering. Such suffering results from attempts on our part to exercise traditional power by dominating, judging and separating.

"We are disturbed not by what happens to us, but by our thoughts about what happens...Nothing external can disturb us. We suffer only when we want things to be different than they are."

~Epictetus, *Encheiridion, V*

Marianne Williamson enlarges this point in *Illuminata: A Return to Prayer*: "There is an old cliche, 'You can see the glass half empty, or you can see it half full.' You can focus on what's wrong in your life, or you can focus on what's right. But whatever you focus on, you're going to get more of. Creation is an extension of thought. Think lack, and you get lack. Think abundance, and you get more."

This idea is the elder sibling of what social psychologists call the "saying-becomes-believing" effect. When we speak or write on behalf of a certain point of view, we come to believe that point of view (positive or negative) more strongly. How we think, what we say and how we behave directly effect how we *feel*, and we can use this knowledge to help ourselves avoid suffering and become the people we've dreamed of being. Similarly, like some kind of behavior- or cognitive-therapy, wearing the Shirt of Flame reduces our self-defeating patterns, or *schemas*, and co-created suffering (induced by our own attachment to ideas of what we're not getting and the ways we are abused or disappointed) by encouraging us to relinquish our 'victim mind' and interact with self and others in positive ways.

Positive thoughts, words and actions are the only way for us to develop communion with others—true Power. With or without "a model for how the river should be," the tree in Ram Dass' example cannot *effect* the river. The tree cannot exert any external force on the river [traditional power] and has no internal influence because it is not part of the river [genuine Power]. We LGBT people, on the other hand, are part of human societies and cultures, and so we have potential for the genuine Power that can change our river's course.

SELFISH ALTRUISM

Extricating ourselves from the thoughts that cause our existential suffering—"society isn't treating me as it should" and all the afflictive emotions that come up with such thoughts, including alienation, disappointment, anger, grief, malaise and so on—does not mean that LGBT people should just pretend that nothing is wrong. We certainly can't deny that we believe in healthier ways for society to function and we can't stop working to create positive change. The motivation for our activism is simply re-languaged:

> We do not engage in social change work because we lack
> anything; our activism is an expression of our desire to
> help ourselves and others achieve genuine happiness and
> avoid suffering.

We are conscious of the selfish component of our work—that we desire the cessation of our own suffering and the development of our inner capacity for genuine, long-lasting happiness (and what could be wrong with that?). At the same time, without deep compassion for self and others, and for the natural world, we cannot behave in ways that develop communion, trust and understanding.

We extend our compassion and love into activism as part of our work to improve ourselves and our circumstances, as well as the circumstances of others. If we are going to successfully establish the Beloved Community, every one of us—YOU—must participate in this very personal work. A lot of us will have to let go of the pervasive idea that

"It's being taken care of by others—I just want to have a good time!"

Of course, having fun and enjoying life are very important! However, many of the things we consider fun are really things we do to try to escape from consciousness of our circumstances. For example, many people watch TV or drink alcohol to avoid thinking about their lives. Such activities, although enjoyable in moderation, are not actually helpful in pursuing genuine happiness, health and freedom. In fact, when looked at head-on, a lot of experiences we typically think of as fun have negative physical and psychological consequences for us on our human quest to achieve happiness and avoid suffering. 'Fun' is not helpful if it sabotages our personal and social evolution. It's not a matter of right and wrong, but a question to be asked of each action: "Will the outcome of this action serve me and who I say I am and who I want to become?"

The very public, hard work of LGBT activist organizations and lobbyists contributes to the perception that others are taking care of social change for us, that we need do nothing but write them a check every once in awhile and show up for their parties and marches. Obviously, their work is vital and needs our support, but alone, it's just not enough.

THE BIG LIE OF LGBT ACTIVISM

The kinds of organized Lesbian, Bisexual, Transgender and Gay activism we use today can never get us more than partway to our goal to create a society in which queers are safe, respected and equally valued. Too frequently, as we've already discussed, LGBT activism actually harms both straights and queers, psychologically, physically or spiritually, forcing both sides away from our goal instead of *toward* it.

We have to be careful, because the ways we choose to *enjoy* life can have the same affect, pushing us further away from what we truly want. In other words, there is a gap between the results we desire and what results are even possible if we keep doing only what we've been doing.

All of us, whether we consider ourselves activists or not, must recognize that our oppression, like a wall, is two-sided, not one-sided. Our focus must be turned inward and outward at the same time, but the only way we'll be able to hold both in mind gracefully is if we stop clinging to thoughts, beliefs and behaviors that limit our attention and cause us suffering. This is why self-control and self-knowledge are inherent in our Power. We have to examine the ways in which we participate in our own oppression.

How many of us have walked down Main Street or through the park with a partner and not grabbed our beloved's hand? For how many candlelit dinners in fine restaurants have we settled for eye contact from opposite sides of the table? How much of our time do we spend with the eyes in the back of our heads wide open, afraid to fully express ourselves for fear of attack?

The answers? Too many. Too much.

Start small and just challenge yourself to observe the ways you think. In the examples just given, although there is an atmosphere of oppression that is sometimes present in public, and certainly there are situations in which it would be unsafe to do so, *most of us actually oppress ourselves* by not grabbing that hand, cupping that waist, offering that peck or special smile, or by only frequenting queer establishments. We do the oppressors' hardest work for them by allowing ourselves to be boxed in. We assume the worst and that keeps us from our best.

You, yes, YOU, deserve a full, joyful and abundant life filled with Truth, Beauty, Freedom and Love, but if you wait for someone else, somebody "over there," to give it to you on a platter—it ain't gonna happen. You have to claim it for yourself.

A great example of claiming space is also one of my favorite memories from when the Rev. Fred Phelps' family (famous for www.godhatesfags.com) visited Ann Arbor, Michigan, in February 2001. My partner dropped me off near the University of Michigan early so I could prepare for my silent prayer vigil sitting among the Phelps family holding their "God Hates Fags" signs.

"If you always do everything exactly as you've always done, you'll always get exactly what you've always had."

~ proverb

The first thing I saw after I got out of the car was an image more powerful than watching hundreds of same-sex couples make out in the university commons later that day, more powerful than any speech I heard: I saw two young, punk men striding confidently across South University Avenue holding hands. What I didn't see was any hint of self-consciousness; maybe a bit of defiance, true (the green mohawk was a clue), but I didn't see a sideways glance, not a hesitation. Just the inspiring courage to walk the world without masks.

CLARITY

> "Ultimately, human intentionality is the most powerful force on the planet."
>
> ~ George Leonard

So the source of our real liberation lies inside each of us individually, and within us as a queer community. Ultimately, yes, straight people, society and institutions will have to change—no question about that. Yes, working toward that legitimation is worthwhile, and all of us should honor and do all we can to support our sisters and brothers who undertake that great labor.

At the same time, though, just as there is another side to our oppression, we need to find the other side of our activism: *liberation*. If same-gender-loving and Transgender people really want to be free, we have to develop Clarity of Intention about achieving our freedom. This means holding the intention to be free higher than lesser desires.

For example, we may experience the understandable desire to feel secure and safe although the drive toward happiness and freedom demands some measure of risk, like coming out publicly. It's like saying that we want a diet based on regular cupcake intake in order to reach a healthy weight! Each of us must make clear distinctions between activities that move us toward the goals of freedom—to live with integrity, equal rights and opportunity, and without fear—and those that push them further from us.

WHERE FEAR HAS TAKEN US

Many adversaries of the LGBT rights movement still pull out images from ACT-UP and OUTRAGE direct actions to 'put the fear of God' into the public. (And to scare millions of dollars from their wallets!)

Many good-hearted straight people were shocked enough by our activists' behavior to close their hearts and minds to us indefinitely, and some were even motivated to directly oppose LGBT civil and human rights. Many more, already predisposed to prejudice by upbringing or belief system, had their fear and horror exacerbated by—some would say caused by—the inflammatory rhetoric of right wing leaders who told them that queers wanted to rape them and their children and destroy everything they hold dear in the world.

Whatever the origination of their antagonism, we are experiencing the effects of their pain and fear in city councils and school boards, religious denominations, social service agencies, clubs, leagues and associations across the country as these individuals attempt to block with rules, laws and ordinances any hope we have for equal treatment under the law.

Just because the *kind* of grassroots activism that some queers undertook had negative consequences doesn't mean that local, grassroots activism *itself* can be abandoned. We can learn from and honor our queer history while at the same time transcending it. Once we've developed Clarity of Intention to liberate ourselves, and if we really want to be free, each of us must work for freedom where we are, in the communities where we live our lives, by putting on the Shirt of Flame.

Nowadays, media and political work sometimes seem to have all but replaced the fiery grassroots LGBT activism of the last thirty years, and without effectively addressing the injury done by our traditional power-oriented activists. Of course, media and politics make important inroads toward widespread public understanding of and empathy with queer people and issues. However, these methods do not usually make allowances for heterosexuals' *future shock*. Not only are they usually impersonal, they also offer no consideration of heterosexuals' rate of adaptivity or the lag between that rate and the rate at which our activists have pushed for change.

LGBT people and our Allies can help establish the Beloved

Community if we use new methods to create change at the grassroots level. We need methods like the ones outlined in these pages that are not only complementary to our concurrent educational and political efforts but also provide a viable alternative to the "parrot-poking" means used by some of our activists.

These alternatives must be both opposite and antidote to the means of aggression, intimidation and violence the LGBT rights movement has frequently employed in the past. At the same time, they should directly increase our individual and collective health and help heal the wounds of future shock.

Such a 21st century queer activism will directly enable the vast number of individuals who have shut their minds and hearts against us in fear or horror and those others, our inactive allies, who sympathize but do not help, to permanently expand their thinking to include Gays, Lesbians, Bi-affectionate and Transgender people in the promise of freedom.

We must inform our actions with a newfound sense of connection to society. After all, we're not seeking to *overcome* society—we seek to become society, not through acclimation or homogeneity, but using mindfulness and the genuine Power of communion. These are the greatest tools in our new arsenal. What are they? They are the light and heat of our Shirts of Flame, the bright and transformative power of Love.

"Do I not destroy my enemy when I make him my friend?"

~Abraham Lincoln

LOVE VERSUS DOMINATION

Practicing Love in our LGBT activism has a broad social affect because the will to Love requires the repudiation of the will to dominate, the rejection of temptations to traditional power. Love, as an action, moves toward communion instead of domination, and fraternity instead of patriarchy (or matriarchy, for that matter). This very renunciation of domination is part of what makes Love radical.

Love incontrovertibly rejects hierarchical patterns of domination that are deeply rooted in our culture, in favor of holonic structures in which every part, or *holon*, is valued as an indivisible element of the larger whole.

Arthur Koestler was the first to use the term "holon" to describe an entity that is itself a whole and at the same time part of another whole. For instance, an atom is a whole atom but also part of a whole molecule, which is itself a whole molecule and also part of a whole cell, which is also part of a whole organism, and so on.

This sequence of development or 'stack'—atom to molecule to cell to organism, and so on—is called a natural hierarchy, an evolutionary order of increasing wholeness and inclusion. Each new whole includes all the constituent holons that make it up, and at the same time transcends the sum of those parts. That is why we say that evolution "includes and transcends."

In order to differentiate between a natural hierarchy and a pathological or dominator hierarchy (traditional power, again), and because a natural hierarchy is really just an evolutionary stack of holons, we call it a *"holarchy."*

Pathological or dominator hierarchies occur when one holon decides it wants to be only a whole and not a part—like a cancer cell dominates a lung, or a patriarchal demagogue dominates a society, or a needy ego dominates an individual's life. Like the movement of Fear, this is always a move toward separation instead of communion.

One of the twenty tenets of holons is that they all must maintain their *wholeness* and their *partness*. Each holon has to maintain its own individuality, its own autonomy, its own agency. If it does not it ceases to exist. So one of the fundamental characteristics of a holon is its agency, which is a capacity to maintain its own wholeness despite outside pressures which otherwise would destroy it.

At the same time, a holon is not just a whole fighting to maintain its agency. It is also part of another system, some other wholeness. So, it simultaneously has to fit into its place as part of something else or it drifts out of the holarchy and ceases to exist.

What happens when you remove one Queen from the cellar of a house of cards? The house of cards falls into a clump of numbers and faces. If one kind of holon is destroyed or removed from a holarchy, the greater whole decomposes into its subholons. For the sake of argument, say we destroy all the molecules in the universe. All cells and organisms, everything molecules were part of, would also be destroyed, while atoms and subatomic particles would remain healthy. The whole always transcends the sum of its parts, but its existence also depends on the consistency of those parts.

It is a kind of Love, then, that heals the break where the diseased holon attempts to separate or dominate, that puts the dominator back in its proper alignment in the holarchy. The genuinely creative Power of that kind of Love is what we're after.

THE FIFTH ELEMENT

"Power," a young Navaho medicine man told Carolyn Raffensperger of the Science and Environmental Health Network, "Power is when you have the ability to speak with all the animals and plants and they have the willingness to speak to you." The external component of our Power is a result of *communion*, not domination, *healing* division, not causing it. The essence of communion is communication enabled by the experience and action of Love.

The word "love" has been thrown around a lot in the last fifty years, and rarely does it mean the same thing to different people at the same time. Most of us were raised to confuse Love with care, physical intimacy and, in all-too-frequent dysfunction, with abuse or neglect.

Many LGBT people have particular trouble giving and receiving love because of mistreatment by our families of origin. Those who taught us much of what we know of love, and those who were *supposed* to love us longest and best, too often rejected us because of our sexual orientation or gender identity.

Without knowing capital-'L' Love, we do not learn what it really means to love, nor how to love one another, whether in *philia* (friendly love), *eros* (intimate love), or *agape* (general love not based on relationship). Unable to understand or practice love in our own lives on a personal, micro-level, we are also unable to induce loving behavior and policies on a macro-level, societal scale. Is it any wonder our social holarchy is in turmoil?

WHAT IS LOVE?

> "Love is freedom. Where love resides freedom resides. Love and freedom are the same energy...Love is also truth. Joy is the essence of who you are. Love is freedom, truth and joy. The greatest of them is freedom. Freedom to be, have and choose."
>
> ~ Neale Donald Walsch in *White Crane Journal*

In order to understand how Love will help Lesbian, Gay, Bisexual and Transgender people create the Beloved Community, we must begin with a shared definition of Love. Taking a cue from bell hooks' book *All About Love: New Visions* and M. Scott Peck's *The Road Less Traveled*, Love is "the will to extend one's self for the purpose of nurturing one's own or another's holistic growth."

In practice, this means exercising care, affection, recognition, respect, commitment, trust and concern, as well as open and honest communication, with those for whom one feels the will to love, with the simple goal of one's own and others' physical, mental, spiritual and social well-being.

Love requires:

1. Care	5. Commitment
2. Affection	6. Trust
3. Recognition	7. Concern
4. Respect	8. Open and honest communication

We must shift away from thinking about love as a feeling. Like other emotions and sensory experiences, love-as-feeling is transitory. Emotions arise without conscious guidance and swirl around and evaporate. Feelings can be observed, but not controlled. Love-as-feeling certainly exists, but because of its instability and characteristic loss of self-control is not a reliable tool for building peaceful, harmonious relationships. So, rather than heeding the beck and call of each new emotion to fly or collapse, we simply name what we're feeling and pay attention.

For example, I sometimes became angry while sitting in my *tonglen* vigil among Fred Phelps' family. Instead of giving them a piece of my mind, I just acknowledged that anger was manifesting in me, and then I sat and observed my anger as its heat subsided and transformed into intense compassion. We can do this with any emotion, but it's especially important that we undertake this simple practice when afflictive emotions like anger, despair, jealousy, craving and delusion come up.

Even our unpleasant emotions are part of us. We must train ourselves to deal with them in healthy, constructive ways lest they keep us from establishing the Beloved Community. Also, it's a good idea to have a trusted friend or therapist with whom one can explore the meaning of one's experiences, since other ways of venting—like primal scream therapy, bitching or hitting a pillow—are actually rehearsing negative, aggressive behavior.

Love is the will to extend one's self for the purpose of nurturing one's own or another's holistic growth.

LOVE-AS-ACTION

Under our new definition, we are only loving when we are either taking action (or are prepared to take action) by extending ourselves to nurture self or others. We are not loving when we are just liking, enjoying, or appreciating, and certainly not when hating, abusing or neglecting.

When we examine our intimate relationships—familial, fraternal, romantic and sexual—under this definition of Love, we may be confronted with a startling lack of genuine Love in our lives. Those who care for us, and those for whom we care, do not always treat us with Love—with the intention to nurture our holistic growth. We may discover that we aren't offering them care, affection, recognition, respect, commitment, trust, concern, or open and honest communication, either. We may even find that we have not been treating *ourselves* with Love.

However, the nature of Love is to extend itself, so when we make the choice to behave lovingly in our relationships, we set in motion a chain reaction that usually leads to increased loving behavior on all sides. Of course, the karmic return of Love to the lover will not necessarily come "from the sources you've poured yours into/ maybe not from the directions you are staring at," as the Bjork song warns, but practicing Love without expectation of a particular result will at least increase one's self-knowledge, self-mastery and inner peace. It just might transform your life and every life around you.

The practice of Love encourages us to be gentle with ourselves, with others and with a universe that may not return Love to us in the ways or from the directions we would prefer. To practice genuine Love involves releasing our attachments to particular outcomes: we do not act just to achieve a certain outcome or result; first and foremost we act to nurture and to relieve suffering. Although we will not stop desiring specific outcomes, we may come to appreciate that, as Buddhists say, "The path is the goal."

"Love is, in fact, an intensification of life, a completeness, a fullness, a wholeness of life...Life curves upward to a peak of intensity, a high point of value and meaning at which all its latent creative possibility go into action and the person transcend himself or herself in encounter, response, and communion with another. It is for this that we came into the world—this communion and self-transcendence. We do not become fully human until we give ourselves to each other in love."

~ Thomas Merton, "Love and Need"

OURS FOR THE TAKING

What is most important is that queers begin to Love, genuinely and deeply, but an intention to Love requires us to see our relationships clearly. We tend to confuse Love with care, attraction, awe, pleasure and cathexis (the process by which another becomes important to us by our investing emotionally in them).

While relationships based on care, attraction, awe, pleasure and cathexis may be intensely enjoyable, and may meet some of our holistic care needs, they are not inherently Love relationships. By applying our working definition and basic understanding of Love, however, such relationships may be deepened and transformed into amazing Love relationships in which basic needs are not only met, but also gloriously exceeded. Individuals' very beings and identities can be challenged and opened by the presence of capital "L" Love.

Because we have defined Love as the "will to extend one's self," Love is largely a choice. Love requires a conscious or unconscious decision to extend one's self to nurture one's own or another's growth. This Love is not something that just mysteriously happens, or which we stumble and fall into like a tiger trap.

This idea directly challenges the popular and socialized notion that Love is outside our control, that we spontaneously and inexplicably 'fall in love.' Seeing Love as outside our sphere of influence is a trick of the mind that absolves us to some extent of our responsibility for being loving people. In fact, as an action, Love is very much within our control.

After initial attraction and cathexis, we make the decision to extend ourselves to nurture the other or not. Even in family relationships, we are conditioned to believe that Love is simply an automatic feeling instead of a choice revealed through care, affection, recognition, respect, commitment, trust, concern and open and honest communication. It's particularly easy to confuse care and affection with Love, since those are the most common elements of Love that do make it into family relationships. Also, many of us cling to the idea that our families are loving despite extremely unloving patterns of behavior that may be acted out in those relationships.

LOVE & ABUSE

Love and abuse are antithetical under our definition of Love. You cannot reconcile the two in one relationship and call it loving. As bell hooks put it: "You can care for me Monday, Tuesday, Wednesday, Thursday, and abuse me on Friday and, although you have not stopped caring for me, you do not love me if you abuse me."

Any abuse is an insult to basic humanity. One may look at a personal relationship under the magnifying glass of our definition of Love and find that one is the recipient of persistent mental, physical, sexual or spiritual abuse. Depending on the level of the individual's commitment to transform the relationship, therapy, intervention or extrication may be chosen to end mental or spiritual abuse.

If reasonable measures taken to eliminate the unwanted behaviors have been unsuccessful—or immediately if the abuse is physical or sexual—to act out of Love for self, the abused should consciously extricate him-or-her self from the abusive situation and/or from the unloving relationship.

One might also realize that one is the *perpetrator* of cyclical abuse. Such a one must be careful to not adopt an "Abuser" self-identification, but instead affirm a "Lover" identification and consciously take steps to heal one's maladaptive thought patterns and correct one's harmful behavior. Besides formal therapy, a simple practice of developing awareness of one's internal activity will be helpful—noticing anger, pain, fear, inadequacy and other afflictive emotions when they arise, and working to experience them without repressing them or acting out.

Evaluating our relationships in the light of Love is mostly difficult because we all want so badly to believe that we have always been loving and loved. The prospect of deep consideration of our relationships, past and present, can be frightening. Some things, we may think, we don't want to know! The truth is that we cannot move forward without doing our 'Love-homework.' Still, years of therapy are not necessary before putting on the Shirt of Flame; only the abilities to discern Love from not-Love and to act accordingly are necessary.

WHY LOVE?

Intentional, enlightened, loving action must be the heart of our 21st Century LGBT activism for three reasons:

First, loving action is the only way forward that is healthy for us. Any approach not grounded in Love damages us in mind and body, endangers our happiness, and threatens our chances for the long-term success. "Anything that promotes feelings of love and intimacy is healing," Dr. Dean Ornish writes in *Love and Survival: The Scientific Basis for the Healing Power of Intimacy*. "Anything that promotes isolation, separation, loneliness, loss, hostility, anger, cynicism, depression, alienation, and related feelings often leads to suffering, disease, and premature death from all causes."

"The time we spend with our loved ones, the quality of our relationships, the strength of our communities, and the openness of our hearts are major determinants not only of the quality of our lives but also the quantity—our survival."

~ Dr. Dean Ornish, essay in
Imagine: What America Could Be in the 21st Century

Second, as we have discussed, we cannot develop communion (genuine Power) without the care, recognition, respect, commitment, and open and honest communication that come with love-as-action.

Finally, taking intentional, enlightened, loving action and educating the public about the antithetical nature of Love and abuse deprives our adversaries of their usual claim that they love LGBT people, just not what we do: "Love the sinner, hate the sin." They cannot claim to Love us while they continue to use misleading and violent rhetoric and lies to attempt to diminish our value, refuse us personal integrity and security, deny us our spiritual traditions, or abuse us in any way. By focusing the conversation and our actions on Love, we also stop enabling our adversaries to sexualize us by implying that the issue of our inalienable civil and human rights is an issue of with whom and how we share physical intimacy, or whether or not we conform to gender stereotypes.

As W.B. Yeats wrote:

> They have spoken against you everywhere,
> But weigh this song with the great and their pride;
> I made it out of a mouthful of air,
> Their children's children shall say they have lied.

— GENIUS, POWER AND MAGIC —
by Ko Imani

From *Goko: The FIRE IN THE LAKE Newsletter*
www.fireinthelake.com

"Let timid doctrinaires depart from among us to carry
their servility and their miserable fears elsewhere. This
people is its own master. It wishes to be the brother of
other peoples, but to look on the insolent with a proud
glance, not to grovel before them imploring its own
freedom."
~19th Century Italian revolutionary, Giuseppe Garibaldi

If you've been paying attention, you've noticed that the Religious
Right has begun to invoke the protection of diversity, tolerance and,
astonishingly, liberalism to support the expression of their anti-gay position. For the health of our society, perhaps it's time to clarify the proper social function of these pseudo-progressive mantras.

Not unlike the members of the Religious Right, Western society as
a whole has fallen victim to a misunderstanding of some of our central
tenets. Ideals at the heart of modern society—namely liberal pluralism,
expressed by honoring diversity—have been almost criminally reduced
to the toleration of all views.

Generally, this modern view claims that no view is inherently better
than another. The Ku Klux Klan has as much right to express itself as
the Anti-Defamation League, and woe befall the one who suggests otherwise. Taken to the extreme, Princess Diana and Jack the Ripper are
put on equal footing! According to this feeble egalitarianism, this political correctness, all views are to be cherished as an example of our "rich
diversity."

Notice that only this liberal pluralism itself is superior. It claims to
reject all hierarchy while affirming its own position on top of the heap.
"No view is better than another, except mine" is an inherent contradiction. This may be the official position, but it's hypocritical and inac-
curate.

In fact, the universe is made up of rankings. Everything is not equally part of the whole because everything is a holon that is part of a holarchy, a ranking of degrees of wholeness. Some things are more whole than, are higher than, others.

The views of the Nazis, for example, are part of the holarchy of human development, but a pathological version of a low level of development. Their worldview does not include or transcend very much, and, as an additional bonus, sabotages the possibility of the higher development of its adherents, not to mention threatening the development of those it rejects and attacks. Such worldviews are pathological because they cripple the evolution of human development.

If we look at the holarchy of morality, we see a movement from preconventional (infantile survival) to egocentric (individual needs), to conventional (social normality) and ethnocentric (tribal mythology), to postconventional (personal achievement), to worldcentric (attending to the well-being of all) and beyond. Attitudes that reject, attack and divide can occur at most levels of moral development, but those of the KKK, the Nazis and the Religious Right are arrested in their development at or below the ethnocentric level.

Of course, most of the Religious Right does not (I hope) want to put same-gender-loving, bi-attractional and gender-queer people into concentration camps like Nazis did. The majority of them are not advocating enforcing Levitical law. They're probably not interested in burning crosses on our lawns.

At the same time, the right to free speech, the right to express oneself and one's belief system or worldview, must exhaust itself the moment one begins to cause harm. The evolutionary mantle of diversity, liberalism and tolerance cannot shelter pathology, especially when pathology is camouflaged in spiritual drag, and especially in the public education of our children. If modern society continues to endanger its development by defending the value of expressions of low-level, pathological worldviews instead of healing and correcting them, disaster looms.

It's time that we grow up and put our amazing human genius to work discerning that which is truly helpful to human development from that which imperils it. We have to use our miraculous power-to-choose in defense of the possibility of being more wholly human, and each of us must excavate the genuinely creative magic that lies within every human heart: our magical ability to Love.

> "Whatever you can do or dream you can, begin it. Boldness has genius, power and magic in it. Begin it now."
>
> ~ Johann Wolfgang Goethe

BEYOND AESOP

Combine Love with the Universal Ethical Standard discussed earlier and we derive an effective and revolutionary guide for behavior in relationships, society and activism—a new collective morality:

> *An ethical, moral act is an action taken to extend one's self in order to nurture one's own or another's holistic growth toward well-being, fulfillment, and genuine, enduring happiness, or to help oneself or another to reduce or avoid suffering. An ethical, moral act inevitably includes elements of caring, affection, respect, recognition, commitment, trust, concern, and open and honest communication.*

Such morality is not exclusive to homophiles or heterophiles of any gender. Rather, this morality of Love offers the potential for a truly harmonious, democratic and liberating existence for everyone. Widely adopted, this moral standard would level the playing field, refusing to allow anyone to claim the moral high ground based on their particularized morality, and placing emphasis instead upon the goals and means of behavior. For example, a condemnation of homosexually active men as immoral based on 5,000 year-old tribal religious practices (and disputed ones at that) would not be able to garner public support or effect public policy if this new morality of Love was the dominant social paradigm.

In the new paradigm, no one would pay attention to the Religious Right's shouting about "abominable sexual sin" because the majority of society would no longer be sympathetic with their incidental model for morality. Naturally, it would also help if bi-affectional and same-gender-loving people were renowned for acting morally, with the intention to nurture, and known for treating other people with caring, affection, respect, recognition, commitment, trust, and concern, and for engaging in open and honest communication.

MISTAKING THE MASK FOR THE FACE

Of course, it's never that simple. As we apply the template for a morality of Love outlined above, we must avoid the tendency to take appearances for reality. This is very difficult, as we have been trained to judge others by how we perceive their behavior. In truth, however, we can never, despite our best informed guesses, know another's heart; the fundamental determinant for ethical, moral, *loving* action is nurturing *intention*, not positive results.

Sometimes you can act with the best of intentions but something bad happens anyway, like giving an adorable kitten to a friend whom you don't know is deathly allergic.

Sometimes the results of our actions appear harmful, but in the end have positive outcomes, for instance, if I shove an elderly woman down in the street, it might upset her before she realizes I pushed her out of the path of a bullet.

Actions may seem outwardly positive, but be motivated by selfish or dishonest intentions, like a politician kissing a baby at a press conference.

Only the one who takes the action can deeply know their actual intentions; the rest of us can merely speculate. The possibility of disparity between inner life, or intention, and actions or perceived results necessitates a commitment to honesty, a willingness to believe the best of others, and trust.

Trust is one of the characteristics of Love, but real trust cannot exist in a relationship where honesty is not forthcoming. One may trust whether or not that trust has been earned, and certainly should begin relationships with the anticipation of trusting the other. Possessing a willingness to believe the best of others means that, in the absence of their personal testimony or similar 'inside information,' we refuse to assign the worst of intentions to others, even to those whose actions we abhor.

Instead, it is helpful when developing relationships, especially impersonal relationships in which we may not have direct access to the other, to leave a space in our thinking for the possibility that the other (and especially the adversary) may be acting with good intentions. We assume nothing, but rather have a "don't-know mind" about the other's intention. We create a space for the possibility of positive intention by:

1. Admitting that we cannot know the other's mind or heart for certain, and,

2. Developing a conscious trust in her or his innate human desire to achieve happiness and avoid suffering.

Making that kind of human connection helps us treat others with Love, which allows for potential communion with them. This is the real 'benefit of the doubt.'

At the same time, naivete will not help establish open communication, commitment, respect, or any other aspect of a loving relationship. A prerequisite for truly loving relationships, personal or public, is honesty. Where there's no truth, there's no Love.

Indeed, lying, misrepresentation and dishonesty only breed disrespect and undermine concern, caring and affection. If Lesbian, Gay, Bisexual and Transgender people are to build our genuine Power and establish the Beloved Community by developing loving relationships with one another, with straight society, and even with our adversaries, we must first take care to exercise our will to Power exclusively to nurture our own or others' well-being, without malice or other negative motivations or intentions. This will remove any need for dishonesty about our intentions and will help develop trust. Second, we must work to transform *ourselves* so that we are more readily disposed to the will to nurture.

THE RIGHT TO I

Our own disingenuous behavior should concern us more than our adversaries' false witness. At least if we're focused on changing ourselves we're putting our attention on something we can control! Truth is an integral part of living consciously; one we cannot escape, deny or avoid if we are to be successful change agents, or, for that matter, lovers.

First and foremost, to put on the Shirt of Flame requires the courageous honesty to come out and self-identify as Lesbian, Gay, Bisexual or Transgender. The labels themselves are unimportant, of course, but the commitment to live and love openly without shame or fear is vital.

Although it is not necessary to come out to behave lovingly in some ways, embarking on this journey to find lasting happiness, health and freedom by transforming self and society with the Shirt of Flame requires honesty that is:

- Complete,
- Conscientious, and
- Non-Aggressive.

In order to create a mutually respectful Love relationship with straight society, we must treat everyone—straight people and institutions, adversaries, allies, and each other—with care, affection, recognition, respect, commitment, trust and concern, and open lines of genuine, compassionate communication with them. This path demands that Lesbians, Gay men, Bisexuals and Transgender people speak and act from a space of *Complete* openness and truth about who we are and whom we love. We begin by living as openly ourselves, without the destructive self-censorship of fear and shame.

An e-mail frequently forwarded around the Internet says, correctly, "If you want to live in a world where you can put your partner's picture on your desk, put her picture there. If you want to live in a world where you can hold your partner's hand on the street, hold his hand," and so on. In other words, to a large extent, we create our own experiences. Like we've already discussed, we deny ourselves many of the experiences that we blame others for refusing us.

Most LGBT people have an unfortunate hypersensitivity to scrutiny and attention. We are often afraid to publicly violate taboos of public space. Mohandas Gandhi wrote, "When a man submits to another through fear, he does not follow his nature but yields to brute force." When queer people submit to the invisible specter of danger, we defer to a psychological "brute force," but sometimes that's in our best interests. We are all aware that public displays of same sex affection and gender variance, in particular, can literally be dangerous in certain situations or locations, so we each rely upon our own best judgment, comfort level and time-table. This is what is meant by *Conscientious* honesty.

The *Non-Aggressive* aspect of our honesty is rooted, again, in our choice of the will to Love over the will to dominate. On the Shirt of

Flame path, LGBT people are not open and honest about ourselves because we want to transform society or because we feel the need to increase queer visibility or because we want to shock or intimidate anyone. Our honesty is not an exercise of domination.

We live openly and honestly because it is the only way to live authentically.

We live openly and honestly because secrets kill.

We live openly and honestly because Bisexual, Transgender, Lesbian and Gay people have the right to personal integrity.

Bisexual, Transgender, Lesbian and Gay people have the right to personal integrity.

LOVE YOURSELF IN ACTION

Such total, mindful and gentle honesty can emerge from self-esteem, or itself foster self-esteem. If you want to live a life of healthy self-Love, you must vigorously embody the active dimensions of self-esteem— identified in Nathaniel Brandon's *Six Pillars of Self-Esteem*—which we'll discuss more a little later:

- Practice living consciously;
- Accept yourself;
- Take responsibility for your thoughts, choices and actions;
- Assert yourself, stand up for yourself and your beliefs, make yourself heard;
- Live purposefully to nurture yourself and others; and,
- Practice personal integrity, honesty and congruency.

As part of the process of becoming more loving to ourselves and deepening our self-esteem, we learn to embrace our wounds and find lessons hidden in the pain. We stop avoiding our pain, we stop distracting ourselves from feeling it, and we acknowledge the areas where we have been hurt or negatively socialized, and by whom or what. More importantly, we move past our pain to begin to construct a way of being that allows the fulfillment of our fundamental goal to achieve happiness and avoid suffering. To live in such a life-affirming way requires us to replace maladaptive patterns of thinking and behaving with thoughts and actions that are congruous with our stated goals and beliefs.

Hope inspires this Love-work—hope for healthier relationships with other people, institutions, the natural world and ourselves. Queers hope to achieve happiness and avoid suffering, and every being on the planet hopes for the same. We are all alike in ambition. This hope is very powerful, embedded in the instinctual and socialized behavior of every living thing. But what is this "happiness" we seek?

THE NATURE OF STORMS

Like "love," "happiness" is a word typically used to describe very different states and experiences by different people at different times. We use the word to refer to experiences of pleasure like hot showers or exquisite desserts, and ideal occurrences, like winning the lottery or being promoted. We tend to use the word "happiness" to describe our high moments, in contrast with the sad, disappointing, depressing troughs of our lives. However, there is no hope of gratifying the senses or the ego permanently— the pleasure or ideal state passes by quickly, and we are hungry again.

When we look deeply at our experiences of happiness based on ideal states or the senses, we find that our happiness is unpredictable and transient. Sensual pleasures—chocolate, Tchaikovsky or sex, for example—are very temporary. M&Ms melt, concertos end and sexual euphoria fades. Money can be spent or stolen, and besides, once people have escaped poverty, studies show no relationship between increased means and greater degrees or occurrences of happiness.

None of this is to suggest that sensual pleasure or ideal states are inherently *bad*, only that such experiences of happiness do not last. It is too easy to become a dilettante of happiness, thinking one can avoid all the sad little troughs that one finds less enjoyable by trying to leap from emotional crest to crest.

The dilettante's quest is never-ending because even once she achieves a certain happiness, like all of us, she *adapts* and the context of the experience changes. The *Costume National* jacket that seemed so perfect a few months ago is now *so* last year. The 50-degree day seems so much warmer in December than it did in October.

Also, psychologist Richard Solomon exposed the "opponent-process principle" which states that emotions trigger opposing emotions. So, in the same way that a skydiver feels incredibly elated after a terrifying jump, the dilettante who reaches a peak happiness cannot avoid an 'opponent-process' experience, the letdown after the high. The higher the crest, the more dramatic the trough. At any rate, trying to repeat or recapture a peak experience sucks much of the intensity from any pleasure derived from it.

Keep in mind, though, that so far we are talking about *sensations* that stimulate *feeling* happy and not talking about happiness itself. We tend to confuse cause (an external experience) and effect (our positive feeling). Remember, sensations and ideal states are unsustainable. We cannot rely on them for our happiness. The source of genuine, long-lasting happiness, just like the source of our true liberation, does not lie somewhere outside of us. The source of genuine, long-lasting happiness lies *within* us.

To clarify, prominent social scientist Dr. David Myers uses the term 'subjective well-being' to refer to people's individual experiences of happiness and life satisfaction. This well-being is subjective because it is defined by each individual's interior reality. Among the many insights in his seminal book, *The Pursuit of Happiness: Discovering the Pathway to Fulfillment, Well-Being, and Enduring Personal Joy*, Dr. Myers outlines four qualities shared by genuinely happy people:

> **1. Self-esteem.** Happy people like themselves.
> *["I'm queer and I love myself today!"]*
> **2. Personal Control**. Happy people believe they choose their own destinies.
> *["I choose my own way and I will not be pigeon-holed or oppressed!"]*
> **3. Optimism.** Happy people are filled with hope.
> *["I believe I can be happy, healthy and free, and I can help make a better world!"]*

4. Extraversion. Happy people are outgoing.
["Hi! What's your name? What's your story?"]

CHOOSING TO LOVE YOURSELF

Okay, that's nice for the happy people, but what about those of us who want to be happier than we are now? What can we do to develop or strengthen these desirable traits?

Well, we must hold onto the idea that we are largely responsible for the state of our subjective well-being. (Obviously some people are exempted from this responsibility, including people with developmental challenges, those with ongoing chemical dependency and individuals with deep psychological scars from severe abuse or trauma.) Like choosing to Love, to a large extent, we can choose to be happy. Dr. Myers quotes William James on this point. "If we wish to conquer undesirable emotional tendencies in ourselves, we must assiduously, and in the first instance cold-bloodedly, go through the *outward* motions of those contrary dispositions we prefer to cultivate." In other words, *we can act ourselves into new ways of thinking.*

"The coward makes himself cowardly, the hero makes himself heroic. There's always a possibility for the coward not to be cowardly and for the hero to stop being heroic. What counts is total involvement."

~ Jean-Paul Sartre

We act ourselves into new ways of thinking all the time when we undertake something new. I may not be the most confident public speaker, but after speaking in front of people with pretended confidence, the element of 'faking it' fades and I become genuinely confident. The same is true with any new role, and, it turns out, with the role of "happy person."

Want to increase your self-esteem and experience of self-determination? Again, start actively embodying the six dimensions of self-esteem: practice living consciously; accept yourself; take responsibility for your thoughts, choices and actions; assert yourself, stand up for yourself and your beliefs, make yourself heard; live purposefully to nurture yourself and others; and, practice personal integrity, honesty and congruency.

Pay more attention to the swiftly passing moments of your life to practice living consciously.

Affirm things you like about yourself, as well as recognizing (without judgment) things about yourself that you like less, to develop self-acceptance.

Act out of the awareness that you are at least partially culpable in many of your life circumstances, and that you have the power to choose differently, in order to understand self-responsibility.

Live with the conscious purpose to nurture yourself and others.

Stand up for yourself to exercise self-assertiveness.

Finally, practice personal integrity, congruency and complete, non-aggressive and conscientious honesty.

You can enhance your feeling of personal control, the strong sense of controlling your life, by doing seemingly little things. Rearrange your office, bedroom or house. Write your Senator, Mayor or newspaper editor about an issue you care about; affirm that you have the power to shape public policy. Instead of indulging in unsatisfying open time, fill your schedule with activities you find enjoyable or believe important. Set high, desirable goals, with progressive, achievable objectives.

To increase your optimism, try to affirm positives instead of negatives. For example, emphasize what you have done, not how much is yet to do. Be generous in praising and encouraging others. Foster the belief that disappointments, setbacks and even failures are due to circumstances that can be changed for the better, not caused by internal faults that are unchangeable. This is an empowering way of outlining shortcomings.

Make eye contact with others; hold it for a few seconds, and then smile. Eye contact increases positive feelings like affection in both participants.

Use language that affirms instead of condemns your circumstances. Author and lecturer Iyanla Vanzant is adept at this kind of relanguaging. Oprah.com explains Vanzant's approach:

> "Often what we say presents our circumstances as harder, lonelier, more terrible than they really are. When we 'language' things that way, we experience our circum-

stances that negatively. Instead, we need to 'relanguage' ourselves. One of the first entries in Vanzant's glossary is 'Cancel Can't.' 'I can't' really means you're unable or unwilling, so you can be honest and say what you mean, which could lead you to say that you are willing. Instead of having a problem, Vanzant suggests that you have a 'divine opportunity.' Problems mean powerlessness, that you have abdicated your personal control. The objectives you need to achieve to reach your goals aren't hard, they're 'challenging.' You're not single. You're 'ready to experience' a new love, a new side of yourself, a new life. And don't be broke, either. You're just 'temporarily out of cash.' It's all the broke people who end up brokenhearted. And beside, you don't want to go on telling the universe that you're busted in any way, shape or form. You're not by yourself, you're 'with yourself.' And finally, don't be afraid. Just admit 'I'm not clear.' Afraid can stop you. Unclear can be... cleared up."

SCISSORS, PAPER, ROCK

When we cultivate the traits of happy people — self esteem, personal control, optimism and outgoingness, as well as realistic goals and expectations—we feel better about our lives and ourselves. So, by changing the way we think, we develop positive thought patterns and healthier ways of handling emotional highs and lows. We feel happier and we are better able to treat others with Love, which in turn increases our genuine Power. At the same time, our happiness will be stronger and last longer if we also create the external circumstances that studies show increase happiness. Dr. Myers identifies five *external* factors that make people happier:

1. Fit and healthy bodies;
2. Supportive friendships that enable companionship and confiding;
3. A socially intimate, sexually warm, equitable committed partnership (like a marriage);

4. Challenging work and active leisure, punctuated by adequate rest and retreat; and,
5. A spirituality that entails communal support, purpose, acceptance, outward focus, and hope.

At the same time, there is hope for a more genuine, lasting happiness—a happiness independent of the senses. This independent happiness is based on equanimity, a certain equilibrium and an inner peace. Genuine happiness comes from the flexibility, gentleness and inner calm that is a consequence of our transformative practice of Love.

While we cannot stop ice cream melting, we can preserve patience. We cannot stop ourselves from aging, but we can develop compassion for ourselves and for other beings. Love, compassion, patience, tolerance, forgiveness, contentment, a sense of responsibility, and a sense of harmony are all self-perpetuating qualities of genuine, lasting happiness. They are the inviolate essence of a peaceful inner existence, which translates into a peaceful outer existence. By also focusing your effort on developing these qualities of inner peace, you, and your encounters with others, will be transformed.

True Love offers us the self-confidence and security to not feel threatened by anyone. Even when confronted by someone behaving destructively, our center of peace and Love need not be shaken. We are not required to participate in their 'stuff.' Wearing our Shirts of Flame, we can be confident that our reactions will always be loving, because that is the only way to nurture our own well-being and theirs.

THE NEAR ENEMY

Acting in order to achieve happiness and avoid or relieve suffering means that we act out of some level of concern for the well-being of self and others. Such action is loving, but is based upon compassion first. Compassion literally means "suffer-together." An experience of empathy for and identification with another person motivates us to act out of our will to nurture, protect and relieve.

At the same time, we are not asked to suffer. Compassion does not demand that we take others' pain onto ourselves. Frequently inspired on some level by a mythology of sainthood, like a traditional reading of the biblical story of Jesus' crucifixion that emphasizes Jesus taking all the sins of the world upon himself, self-martyrdom is common but is in fact a kind of violence against the self. Sacrifice is unnecessary. We must always remember to treat ourselves with Love, as well!

The obvious enemy of compassion is cruelty, but compassion also has a subtle enemy: pity. The distinction between pity and compassion is important because "if someone pours her heart out to us and we pity her, then two people are suffering instead of one," as Ayya Khema writes in *Visible Here and Now*. If we want to reduce the amount of suffering in the world, adding to our own suffering can hardly help!

Surely we shouldn't look *away* from other people's suffering, though, so how can we handle it without pitying them? One thing we can always do that is helpful and causes no harm is deceptively simple: we can stay awake with someone in the hour of her or his suffering. We can *bear witness*.

Genuine compassion is not motivated by pity, but by empathy and identification with others' desires to achieve happiness and avoid suffering. Genuine compassion is independent of emotional attachment based on projection and expectation. We do not act with expectation of a particular result. We do not feel genuine compassion because we project our desires, opinions or impulses onto another; indeed, such projection is one root of the ills striking the LGBT community—our adversaries are too busy attacking their idea of us to interact with us as we really are.

When we are able to compassionately act because we recognize that, like us, another desires to achieve happiness and avoid suffering, when we are able to act with a will to nurture, we act with genuine compassion. Such compassion arises from Love, and such Love from genuine compassion.

Love and compassion are not ephemeral concepts, but active and powerful levers that will enable meaningful social change. The old claim that "if you give me a big enough lever I can move the world," is a clumsy truism. It is more true for us to say that if enough people use enough small levers, the planet will shift. Love and compassion are small levers with enormous impacts. Not only are they our tools for the positive transformation of self and society, but Love and compassion are also exemplars of a global paradigm shift toward integration and communion, the manifestations of which we are only now beginning to recognize.

THE NEXT WAVE

The paradigm, or world-view, of the Enlightenment was the modern, mechanistic view suggesting that the universe was a changeless constant waiting to be mapped by "Man." This world-view held that person and universe were fundamentally separated, and, like an alien cartographer, Mankind's duty as steward of the mysterious universe was to unlock and manipulate its secrets for Mankind's own pleasure and benefit. This paradigm was based on faith in absolutes—black and white, right and wrong, sin and virtue, possible and impossible—and placed human beings on a throne at the pinnacle of a dominator hierarchy, a vertical ranking emphasizing absolutist differentiation without complementary integration.

Later came the post-modern understanding that one cannot separate the cartographer from the map. The mapmaker brings with her to map-making her entire background of knowledge, experiences and opinions, which color her perception of reality, and likewise bias her map. This paradigm arose from doubt in the Enlightenment world-view because of a perceived fluidity of facts—"the one who's looking is perceiving correctly for her." Postmodern physicists even tell us that atoms appear to be actually moved by observation; that the simple act of observing the universe may change the universe.

Because of the suffering caused by prominent dominator hierarchies, postmodernists challenged all absolutism, leading to political correctness and greater inter-religious tolerance, for example. Unfortunately, this effort to keep anyone from overtly dominating others became a fanatical denial of all hierarchies, throwing growth (or *actualization*) hierarchies out with the dominator bathwater. Postmodernism all but eliminated the vertical—ranking one higher than another—and established a kind of horizontal 'flatland' that inhibited real transformation: integration without differentiation.

Now we are moving from this relatively recent post-modern development into a new paradigm that we can see manifesting in our technology and our growing understanding of psychology, physics, systems theory, sociology, ecology, technology, politics and evolution itself. This paradigm is based on communion in the face of doubt and difference, and is rooted in deep empirical and philosophical understandings of the interconnectedness of all life. It is a world-view to which nonviolence particularly belongs, a world-view of Interdependence—the holonic marriage of differentiation and integration.

STRANDS IN THE WEB OF LIFE

> "Interdependence is and ought to be as much the ideal of man as self-sufficiency. Man is a social being. Without interrelation with society he cannot realize his oneness with the universe or suppress his egotism."
>
> ~ M.K. Gandhi

Interdependence is the scientific and philosophical principle that "no one is an island." A scientist might quote Ken Wilber and say that Interdependence means that, "All empirical phenomena are aspects of a unified process." What this means is that every thing in the universe is inexorably bound to every other thing. "Bound" is perhaps the wrong word, because deep understanding of this principle is a freeing experience. For example, grasping that, at a sub-atomic level, we are made of exactly the same stuff as Orion's Belt, the colors of tonight's sunset and a fawn. While this does not implicitly imply that we are phenomenally *the same thing*, Interdependence does mean that we are all part of a single progression; we are *connected* to every thing, through the building blocks of our physical existence, the ripples of our living, the motion of energy under our particles, and by circumstances outnumbering stars. Some people call this idea "At-One-Ment," because it reconciles all differences and separations.

Because every thing is a holon, itself a whole and at the same time part of a holarchy, it's easiest to imagine the principle of Interdependence as a pyramid. An Egyptian pyramid is made up of thousands of huge stones, each of which is its own stone as well as a fundamental part of the greater whole, the pyramid. Growth or actualization hierarchies work in this way, converting heaps of seemingly individual, separate things into wholes, finding integration in fragments, and turning alienation into cooperation.

One aspect of Interdependence that helps us understand it is called "Codependent Origination." Thich Nhat Hanh, whom Martin Luther King, Jr. nominated for the Nobel Peace Prize in 1967, gives a wonderful example in his book, *Being Peace*. For the sake of argument, take a look at the piece of paper on which you're reading these words. Consider it in terms of Interdependence: You would not have this useful piece of paper without the recycling of its previous user, the efforts and effects of its marketers and packagers, the factory workers who pressed the paper, the truck drivers who brought the wood to the factory, the loggers who cut the lumber, the scouts who found the lumber, and all of their ancestors who helped put them in the world and in the circumstances to provide you with this piece of paper. You can even see the trees themselves, the seeds they grew from, the rain and sunlight that helped them grow, the cloud the rain fell from, and so on—all contributing to create and shape this single sheet of paper and get it into your hands.

Recognizing that our circumstances are inseparable from the lives, choices, efforts and histories of so many other people and wonders helps us overcome our feelings of separation from one another, from society, and from the natural world. We frequently think that we LGBT people are born outsiders, that we are predestined to remain alienated from society and culture. We often act with faith that we are irreconcilably distant from our fellow beings and our environment. Interdependence reminds us that this is not true—it is only a misperception under which we choose to labor. The wonderful good news is that we can choose to see our situation, our heritage, our place and our function differently.

WE HAVE SEEN THE ENEMY, AND THEY ARE US

Working with the principles of Interdependence, compassion and Love, LGBT people consciously renounce the perception of our oppressors as enemies. We see how our history, fate and (fortunate and unfortunate) circumstances are linked to theirs. Our "enemies" instead become incredibly important and valuable beings with whom we share a holarchical existence. They are beings whose suffering and joy have dramatic direct and indirect effects on us. Our most vocal adversaries are simply people arrested in the grip of an outmoded worldview based on dominator hierarchies, people whose pain and misunderstanding are (very unfortunately) acted out in increasingly harmful ways.

When we begin to see our enemies in this way, we immediately begin to feel enormous compassion for them, these injured and ignorant people who only want, just like us, to be happy and avoid suffering! They simply do not understand their interdependent connection with us, nor what genuine happiness and love are, nor how to achieve them. They have chosen Fear. They are scared and hurt and acting out their suffering and pain. They cause harm consciously, but they really don't know what else to do or why they ought to do things differently. Many of them actually feel an intense fear that to change their beliefs or behavior, in and of itself, would doom them to eternal suffering. They feel safest where they are, and the information-base they're working from says that they already have all the facts and everyone else is wrong. Still, in the best interests of our well-being and theirs, we must offer our conscious, loving commitment to their happiness and avoidance of suffering. In fact, it is helpful to think of them as if they were our children, whom we love, we teach, we nurture, even when they don't desire or appreciate it.

People, just like actors onstage, always take actions in order to get something—often several things at once. For instance, a talk show host might call LGBT people "biological errors" in order to get publicity, listeners, positive attention (from those who agree with him), and negative attention (from those who disagree), and to feel powerful, smart, influential and important. It would not be hard to look at such a person and imagine a small child, attention-starved and devalued by parents, peers and teachers, trying to get anyone at all to pay attention to him, by any means necessary. Looking at this adult and imagining the poor, damaged child inside him makes one feel like hugging him, not threatening him!

One can do this exercise with anyone who is acting out in a harmful way. Picture the first "enemy" who comes to your mind as a frightened little child and see how your feelings about her or him change. Whether your image is accurate or not does not matter. The goal is simply to change your attitude about your "enemies"—to help you treat them as part of your enormous, interdependent family; to help you treat them with Love, and in a spirit of respect, reverence and reconciliation.

Henry Wadsworth Longfellow wrote that "If we could read the secret history of our enemies,/ we should find in each man's life/ sorrow and suffering enough to disarm all hostility." In that spirit, we must avoid holding grievances against those who oppose us—parents, co-workers, celebrities and strangers, religious and government leaders. We must remember that not only are they just like us, these human beings trying, in the midst of suffering, to achieve happiness and avoid suffering, but at the same time they are also interdependently connected to us in more ways than we can ever hold in mind.

Besides, *they do not see us*—not as we are. They see only their *idea* of who we are. The dangerous-to-the-family, child-recruiting, fundamentally diseased and disordered, god-hating, and highly-organized gay rights movement with its "gay agenda," is their concept. They can only deal with LGBT people as stereotypes and sex acts, not as people as varied and diverse as heterosexuals. They are wrong about who we are and what our goals are, but should we hold their error against them? Of course not. Clinging to pain and ill will does not benefit either party. Our capacity to forgive must be grand.

Forgiving our opponents does not mean that we forget or ignore their harmful words and deeds. Of course we continue to be conscientious and careful—we don't have to place our hand on the stove again and again to prove that, yes, it's really hot! Remembering the harm that others cause does not mean, however, that we withhold our forgiveness.

Our forgiveness arises directly from our compassion for them as confused and suffering beings. We must avoid judging people and holding grudges against them because judgment acts as an agent of holonic separation that destroys our evolutionary potential to include and transcend. When we see what our enemies do not, that by attacking us they are engaged in indirect self-destruction—since, as we have already learned about Interdependence, "What is done to one is done to all, and to me"—our hearts open to them.

Judgment acts as an agent of holonic separation that destroys our evolutionary potential to include and transcend.

When one is acting out of fear, rage or pain, or with a traditional will to power, one is not happy. If one were genuinely happy, one would not be in the grip of negativity and afflictive emotions. Our enemies are not genuinely happy people! Neither are we when we allow our afflictive emotions to dictate our thoughts and actions. It's helpful to think of every form of attack as a cry for Love.

We must choose to be compassionate with our unhappy opponents the way we would be with our children or ourselves when a mistake is made. They either don't know any better or feel powerless to change. Our 'enemies' need us to stretch our hands through their cataract of illusions and make contact. They need our help to really see us. All together, one at a time, we can steal back their hallucination with our Shirts of Flame.

Part of working with Interdependence is seeing others as extensions of ourselves, so that when we are misdefined, insulted and stigmatized by others we can take advantage of that opportunity to work with our own tendencies to pre-judge and define our adversaries in ignorance of their intentions. If we return their fire, we only 'poke the parrot.' Instead, one can smile gently, lean over and touch a feather to their bubble saying, "You can call me whatever you want, describe me however you want, but I AM NOT THAT. Come with me, I will share myself with you."

Our ideas and our adversaries' are in conflict, it's true, but wearing the Shirt of Flame directs us to participate in that conflict without violence of any kind toward any person—including demonizing, insulting, and mocking our enemies. Responding to attack without resorting to violence is called *Non-Retaliation*. To succeed in achieving personal and communal health, if we are to establish the Beloved Community, we must renounce all violence of fist, tongue, and heart. After all, the end is inherent in the means.

"GIVE UP WHAT YOU DON'T WANT. KEEP WHAT YOU DO."

A nonviolent movement in the tradition of Mohandas K. Gandhi and Martin Luther King, Jr., might be simplistically defined as "relentless incarnation of Truth and Love," "mass non-cooperation with evil," "doing justice," or "speaking truth to power." Gandhi used the Sanskrit term *"Satyagraha"* (*"Sat"* meaning "Truth" and *"Agraha"* meaning "Firmness") to describe his nonviolent movement for the independence of India from British rule. He explained nonviolence as the practice of *"Ahimsa"* ("not-harming"), requiring rejection of all physical, verbal and psychological violence.

Derived from this tradition just for Gay, Lesbian, Bisexual and Transgender people, the Shirt of Flame is an experience and a movement based on achieving individual and collective health and happiness by healing internal and external threats to that health and happiness. This is our path to Love, our *"Satyagraha."*

If we are abusing self or others, we are not loving, which means neither are we developing communion. *By abusing self or others, we relinquish Power.* If we act in a way that contradicts what we believe or what we ultimately desire (communion, freedom, respect, health, happiness, avoidance of suffering, etc.), this inconsistency reflects a real dishonesty in our interactions with the world. Without honesty (or perceived honesty), trust is impossible, also making communion impossible. Once you put on your Shirt of Flame, you join a movement that is the congruous, loving, radical, firm and gentle assertion of universal ethical values in the face of unethical and immoral laws, practices, behaviors and ideas that are themselves unjust and engender further injustice.

Every means and technique of violence and destruction leads only to further violence and destruction. Simply from an evolutionary viewpoint, violent means must be eschewed because judgment and elimination are the antitheses of incorporation and transcendence, the trademarks of evolution. Violent approaches attempt to dissolve organized structures into their component elements or factions, and include all forms of attack, whether violence of the heart, tongue or fist.

One cannot incorporate and transcend by dis-integrating or rejecting. To react from fear and/or with an intent to harm, degrade or intimidate leads only in a circle to more violence. Darkness begets darkness in the hearts and minds of self and others in the form of resentment, anger and desire for vengeance, and that interior murk eventually overflows into the world as more violent actions. In most cases, using violence to stop violence only makes more violence.

The end is inherent in the means. So, if the end we desire is to transform our nation into the peaceful, compassionate and inclusive society it dreams of being, we must use means which are proactively peaceful, compassionate and inclusive. To do otherwise is to invite defeat or a corruption of result.

We must be constantly mindful that our goal is not to install a different system of domination in the guise of community. Our goal as LGBT people working with Shirts of Flame is to create a culture in which people of diverse worldviews and experiences can live harmoniously and prosperously. The *Sun Tzu*, or as it is better known in the West, *The Art of War*, calls our means to that end "taking whole."

"TAKING WHOLE": RECONCILIATION WITHOUT COMPROMISE

The 2,300 year-old Chinese book *The Art of War* emphasizes essential generalship and strategy, and its compilation of military wisdom is still widely considered valid and helpful. The manual is used around the world—in corporate boardrooms and movie-making as well as in warfare and conflict resolution. *The Art of War* is frequently misunderstood as a purely Machiavellian explication of deception and domination, but, in true post-modern tradition, it depends on who's looking. The Denma Translation Group, for instance, points out that "Taking Whole" is one of the great themes of the *Sun Tzu*.

In conventional warfare, when one state or emperor attempts to extend his rule over another, The *Art of War* cautions the military strategist to remember that victory is more than just success on the battlefield. Once a battle [a physical exercise to gain traditional power] is won and the soldiers move on, the territory just gained must be held, prisoners contained, peace maintained, and supplies have to get throug' the front lines. If the conflict has been conducted without " whole," there will be dissention and rebellion among the c who are now behind the lines, making ultimate long-te impossible.

The ideal victory happens without battle, "taking whole" the territory of the other by gaining the sympathy and trust of the other's people and—to put it in Shirt of Flame terms—developing communion with them, increasing one's own Power. Then, if the general must move militarily, she moves with the blessing of her enemy's people; they welcome her and simplify her task. In 225 A.D., Chinese strategist Chuko Liang used just such a strategy. Whenever he captured his enemy's troops, they fully expected to be executed. Instead Liang would take off their chains and speak to them of how worried their families must be about them. Then he would send them home to their wives and children with his blessing. The next time the enemy king rallied his troops, they betrayed him and delivered him to Liang, who had generously spared their lives, saying, "It is better to win hearts than cities; better to battle with hearts than weapons." By knowing the environmental and psychological factors that affect victory, the general can do the quiet, precursory work to arrange these factors so that their power becomes available to her, and so, when she acts, she can be assured of victory.

For us LGBT people, this means that precipitous action on our behalf will not have the longevity of result that "taking whole" would. Admittedly, to dwell in chaos and uncertainty requires courage and faith. We will face many challenges while we focus on long-term victory by arranging factors in our favor, starting with ourselves and moving outward to communion and community. However, effective, popular, long-term solutions are vastly more important than resolving immediate conflicts or discomfort. As Baltasar Gracian said:

> "Do something well, and that is quick enough. What is done immediately is undone just as fast, but what must last an eternity takes that long to do. Only perfection is noticed, and only success endures. Deep understanding achieves eternities. Great worth requires great work. So with metals: the most precious of them takes the longest to be refined, and weighs most."

"aster's tools will never dismantle the Master's house."

~ Audre Lourde

Law does not dictate the beliefs and actions of men and women; rather, they dictate Law. If we want to change laws, we must focus on changing the hearts and minds of the people. Our legislative activists and lobbyists should continue their important pursuit of enumerated guarantees for our rights, while the rest of us begin the essential task of arranging the ground for long-term victory on every front. Without our work among the people, their work in legislature cannot ultimately succeed. Another legislature or executive can overturn any short term gains. Only by arranging the ground so that to deny LGBT people any of our human and civil rights is *unthinkable* and *abominable* to a majority of the citizenry can we extend our victories through time.

Some of us have ego issues triggered by the process of "taking whole" inherent in a Shirt of Flame movement. Some will shout (again like Cuba Gooding's character in *Jerry Maguire*) "You're telling me to dance!" A conscious process of community building, 'preparing the ground', may invite the indignant question, "Why should we have to prove ourselves to anybody?" An answer is, of course, "To take our society whole!"

Through our Love and our communion-developing actions, we will open hearts and minds across the board, leading to change at that *causal* level, manifesting in victory: legal protections; equality provisions; and, most importantly, the repudiation of violent and discriminating behaviors. By moving too quickly toward the manifestations of change, we impose our value system upon an ignorant and unprepared public, causing more ill-will, violence, and bitterness. Pushing too much change on heterosexuals too fast is perceived as a threat, a direct attack. Remember, the homeostatic nature of people and systems is to maintain the status quo at all costs, and homeostasis resists all change, positive or negative.

However, if we are willing to take the time to arrange the ground, we can demonstrate and teach a new, healthier method of being together in community, so that, when the manifestations of change gradu occur, they occur with the support of, and because of, the general lic. Like the old proverb says, "If you stand on the porch and ju the stars, you'll fall on your face in the mud. The stairs mus structed first."

BURGEONING

Community-building through Love and pure nonviolence, then, is the best way to healthily induce the long-term, evolutionary transformation of our society, and as LGBT people, the Shirt of Flame is the only way to build the stairs to the ultimate achievement of our goals.

To succeed, we must not just aspire to the name of nonviolence but to its spirit and constant practice. The spirit of nonviolence is centered on unconditional Love, but this means in practice relentless reverence, respect, and reconciliation for and with life in all its forms, particularly in the shape of an enemy, whatever the cost. While this does not immediately disincline our natures to violence, it does mean that when we are motivated (by fear or pain) to violence, our choice is inevitably to act (to speak, to write, to protest) lovingly—with reverence and respect and for reconciliation. It is as if we are each allowed to choose one of three birds to sing our only song from the flexing cage of our ribs: a croaking and pecking bird of spiteful anger; one of judicial, Pavlovian fits; or a bird singing glorious arias of kindness.

Consensus on appropriate, purely nonviolent techniques and then, unified action among scattered LGBT people of conscience are necessary if the forces of life and Love are to surpass society's pandemic of fear, scarcity and greed. All kinds of activists must stop treating symptoms as causes and work together to reform the basic underlying disease of not-love afflicting our people and our world with barely mitigated violence. New adaptive patterns of reverence, respect, and reconciliation will be widely adopted if enough of us model them. Old, violent, maladaptive patterns will be deselected as they are faced down and become universally unacceptable. This is the New Resistance, the "Fire in the Lake." The revolution has not ended, and our 'kairos' to become a part of the body of revolution is here—this is the right time; this is the right moment.

We Lesbian, Gay, Bisexual and Transgender people are like seeds, arded onto parched ground and forgotten, that unexpectedly find the of nourishment and sprout, cracking the dry earth with our blos- and bringing kaleidoscopic and brilliant new life into the waste. sooner do we see the shining sky than we turn our faces to around us, the heat, the wind, the drought. Here there is rock, rock and no water, it seems, for miles. We know instinctively and from experience that this world is very dangerous, very hard, unyielding in its hatred and fear. Injustice against us is evident, not only in the books of law, but in the sneers of children, the turned backs of clergy, the belts of parents, the gauntlets of sidewalks. This is old news. This is known.

Many of us are withered by it. Many shrink into a sleepy half-life just under the soil and wait for cover of night to burgeon. (By the time night comes it will be too late.) Many blossom in defiance—huge scarlet and honey frangipani blooms in a Serengeti sun—and are destroyed. Too many of us become inverted by unwarranted guilt and shame. Many are consumed and turn chameleon-like into colorless and quick secrets.

All of us, however, whether Transgender, Bisexual, Lesbian, Gay or Heterosexual—all discarded seeds are seeds of Love. Love is the hidden source, the spring, the entangled and ancient root no one has seen that nourishes our joy, true evolution, universal compassion and knowledge-in-action. The challenge we face is to let the fertilizing sap of Love flow from our lives' veins into the world without destroying ourselves in the process. You can choose to become a garden.

Only the blazing, empowering armor, conscious or unconscious, named or unnamed, of the Shirt of Flame can preserve us from psychological and social annihilation. Love and respect for self and others invariably deflects the direct and indirect attacks of enemies and rebuts destructive patterns in us and in others. In such Love, too, nests queer people's future emancipation from injustice and the ultimate evolution of society.

Today, modern society's baser functions are everywhere obvious and painful—children killing children, hate crimes and discrimination against minorities, prison construction as the number one industry, drug abuse, child and domestic abuse, poisoned air, water and earth, the eradication of ancient cultures and plant and animal species, sanctions, genocide threats to civil liberties and endless war and so on and on. Today world approaches a turning point decision of such vital importance the futures of all beings on the planet hang suspended in our de Although still fundamentally a choice between Love and Fear, th ing point is made up of infinite smaller decisions and concessions that are already being made at every level of our society. The choice of Fear or Love at every level, in every decision—morning through night in each heart at its every intersection with the world—weights the scale one way or the other.

Of course, one cannot choose Love out of Fear! We may not appear loving and take daring and compassionate actions because we are afraid of what may happen if we do not. On the contrary—we must act because we love life and beauty. We must act now to relieve our suffering and the suffering of others because we recognize the similarity of our conditions and our interdependent relationship. We act, not because "injustice anywhere is a threat to justice everywhere," as Dr. King said (although it is), but because injustice anywhere is unworthy of us, incongruent and unnecessary in a world as abundant and technologically capable as ours. Injustice, torture, hunger, economic disparity, jingoism, war, crime, hatred, most disease, and bitterness quite simply need not be. Such darkness could not remain in the presence of our light, should we all choose to shine.

Here, then, is the new "gay agenda": to become; to be; to live; to evolve; to Love and to help others learn to Love. We come wearing Shirts of Flame to instigate a *Volta*—as in an Italian sonnet, *a change of direction*—in our own lives first, and then, proactively and transitively, for everyone. We will burgeon mindfully, and our wakeful witness will encourage others.

"We must learn to reawaken and keep ourselves awake, not by mechanical aids, but by an infinite expectation of the dawn, which does not forsake us in our soundest sleep. I know of no more encouraging fact than the unquestionable ability of man to elevate his life by a conscious endeavor."

~Henry D. Thoreau

Today we may be Sleeping Beauties, reclined in palaces of dust and [...]n, but we are at the same time Princes, endowed with powers of [...]ulness and action. We will waken, when we waken, as one body [...] morning, to our full splendor and potency. We will wake up as inexhaustible vessels pouring forth renewal onto the dry land.

We Lesbian, Gay, Bisexual and Transgender people declare our intent to transform the wasteland into a peaceful, tolerant, healthy, prosperous, compassionate, culturally and environmentally sustainable society, and our mass dedication to establish that Beloved Community will create the irresistible dynamic force to create it. By dotning Shirts of Flame and becoming love-in-action, we will change the world.

3
THE SHINING ONES

"The need for love and for connection to the community is not a luxury but a basic human need. It is as fundamental as eating, drinking, and sleeping. We ignore it at our own peril."

~Dr. Dean Ornish

GETTING IT ON

"There are thresholds which thought alone, left to itself, can never permit us to cross. An experience is required."

~ Gabriel Marcel

The pianist has stopped playing. Except for the breathing and rustling of the hundred people sitting in the audience, the long hall is silent. A warm light fills the front of the hall, and the flickering candles around the dais make the moment feel sacred. A number of unlit candles rest along the back of the platform. There's an electric expectation in the air, only heightened when the Officiant enters and takes her place at the front of the room.

After a moment's hesitation, music drifts again from the piano as women and men, consecrants dressed in white and red, file quietly up the aisles from some secret spot in another room where they have been preparing themselves for tonight's ceremony. They roll wheelchairs or walk very intently toward the front, obviously focusing on every movement, and finish in a line facing the Officiant, who begins to speak when the music stops.

"We are gathered here to witness and celebrate these Lesbian, Gay, Bisexual and Transgender women and men's commitment to living their best lives by working to help themselves and others find genuine happiness and avoid suffering. They invited you, their family and friends, to be here tonight because they hope to share their best lives with you, and because no one can succeed without the support and love of others. Will you honor their commitment by offering them your love and support?"

A hundred voices say, "We will."

The Officiant looks at each Consecrant and addresses each by name. "I don't know all of you well, but I am so proud of you. I know that you have suffered greatly, in many ways, not least because you are Lesbian, Gay, Bisexual or Transgender. Most people get so crushed by their negative experiences that they never have the courage or wisdom to even consider the life choice you make tonight. You, on the other hand, rise up before us now, strong and vital, to claim your power to create joy and healing, not only in your own life, but in the life of the world. It's so beautiful. You're so beautiful!

"The forces of history and evolution, integrating and transcending, hold you up with their power. There have been other oppressed peoples who have claimed love as you do now, and you come here in their company and in their memory. You, though, are the queer pioneers of a new age. You are the beginning of a new transformational Lesbian, Gay, Bisexual and Transgender movement on the Earth. After you will come centuries of young LGBT women and men, standing where you stand tonight and making the same commitment to create the best life and the best world they can imagine. But you, you are here at the beginning, with all the courage and uncertainty of conception.

"In the legends of Ireland, the Sidhe ["shee"] are beautiful and powerful divine beings who live inside hollow hills. They are sometimes also called "The Good Folk" or simply Fairies. They will ride out from their mounds and fight beside mortals for a just cause, armed with lances of fire and shields of pure white. When you begin your 21st Century LGBT Activism, when you emerge from your closet and comfortable spaces to don your Shirt of Flame and join with others in just causes, you become one of the new Sidhe.

"Tonight, you've chosen to wear the Sidhe's white and red, white to symbolize the purity of your intention and of your highest Self, and red to symbolize your own suffering, past, present and future, and the suffering you will relieve and prevent. The mingling of these symbolic colors on your body may represent the intersection in you of world and Spirit, the reconciliation of your highest Self and your Shadow, your courage to expose your wounds to healing light, or the peace, love and light you bring with you into conflict, pain and darkness.

"Whatever the white and red mean to you, they are a cloth tattoo marking you as one of the Sidhe. They show that you are not only making a personal declaration but you're also joining a community of like-minded LGBT people.

"We, as human beings as well as an LGBT movement, cannot succeed in isolation. We need other people to enrich, support and witness our lives; science has proven that such connections make us stronger, happier and live longer. The Sidhe are one way that we can support, enrich and witness other LGBT people's lives and be witnessed, supported and enriched in turn. The Sidhe community is growing as more and more people discover how wonderful it feels to walk a path of cultivation, transformation, and Love with others of like mind. We're grow-

of cultivation, transformation, and Love with others of like mind. We're grow-ing through groups like this one, and thousands of people making commitments like the one you make tonight.

"Tonight's initiation never ends. You will continue to gather with other Sidhe to recommit yourselves, to share each other's joys and pains, and to work togeth-er to create a Beloved Community, one project at a time. It's the work of a life-time, with rewards and successes we haven't dared to dream of, including a glob-al, intentional and transformational LGBT community.

"In your every loving action, you shall receive our blessing and support, but now, we ask each of you to state your intention."

One by one the Consecrants come forward to face the audience of family and friends and say, "I, [name], come before you to dedicate the rest of my life to doing everything I can to help myself and others achieve happiness and avoid suffering." After each Consecrant speaks, the entire audience declares, "We accept and honor your devotion."

When all Consecrants have spoken, the Officiant goes on. "On this day you formally declare your intent to embody to the best of your ability the attributes of love. What are the attributes of love?"

The Consecrants answer together, "The attributes of love are care, affection, recognition, respect, commitment, trust, concern, and open and honest commu-nication. I will behave in all ways and at all times with an attitude of respect, reverence and reconciliation."

"With this ceremony you claim the responsibilities and possibilities of full par-ticipation in this community and in the global community," the Officiant con-tinues, smiling and looking each Consecrant in the eye. "May you be blessed with a joyful and abundant life. May all good and helpful things flow freely to you and through you: love; health; vitality; wealth; success; recognition; creativity; inspiration; growth; balance; transformation and peace.

"Please name your purpose to this gathering and then come up and light a candle from the central candle, which represents the realm of possible Good. All of us know that the flame you light will burn out in a few hours, but the light of your life will illuminate the dark places of the world forever."

One by one, each Consecrant comes forward and makes a short declaration of one or more areas they feel called to work in: to help farmers grow and sell organic crops; to promote children's rights; to organize a community garden; to become a mentor; to revitalize inner cities; etc. Then she or he solemnly takes *a taper from the front of the dais, lights it from the central candle and sets it in a candleholder before rejoining the others.*

When all of them have stated their intentions and lit their candles, the Officiant concludes. "And so it is. May the world honor you for who you are as well as for what you do. May your life and legacy lay the boundaries of a Beloved Community around the entire Earth. Those of us gathered here, representing this community, this nation and this world, offer you our thanks." She addresses the audience. "And thanks to each of you for the role you have played in preparing these women and men to stand here tonight, dedicating themselves to creating a future unlike the past, a future of true equality, freedom, justice, joy, opportunity, peace and love for all people."

She hands a basket to the Consecrants. "And one last piece of business, so you don't have to walk around wearing white and red all the time! Each of you please take a pin with the Sidhe symbol on it and wear it fearlessly and with pride. Thank you everyone! Enjoy the evening!"

Music starts again from the piano as the Consecrants' families and friends gather around them, hugging and congratulating them and half dancing with them to a reception for the newly inducted members of the Sidhe community.

UNBROKEN

So now you stand on the mountaintop. You've heard the arguments and you've chosen your weapon, the only logical choice, the instrument of Love—the Shirt of Flame. It's a courageous choice as well as an intelligent one, but, what now?

Gandhi called adherents to his nonviolence Satyagrahi, or embodiments of Satyagraha—"Truth"+"Firmness." Our Shirt of Flame includes the traditional nonviolence of Gandhi and King and transcends it, moving in a new direction, so those who choose the Shirt of Flame also require a new identity: *The Sidhe.*

If you choose to participate in one, you may find that a ceremony like the one that opens this chapter is helpful when you dedicate yourself to this path. Such rituals create a transitional context for the life change you're making, and remind both participants and witnesses of the significance of this transition for you, for the lives that intersect with yours, and for the world.

Ideally, such rites-of-passage will become an integral part of life transitions LGBT people go through, especially coming out. Tying this ritual in with coming out could make a big difference in the future well-being of the queer community. Imagine if, as soon as LGBT people stepped out of the darkness of the closet, they were welcomed into a healthy, vibrant and creative LGBT community, instead of receiving the welcome we have been offering the newly out. In the past, people have come out privately and then wandered into the bars, clubs and community centers where coming out's only reception from the LGBT community was, "Oh, now you can openly have sex with us/ date us/ party with us/ lobby with us/ give money to us!"

By installing a ritual of coming out that adds new meaning to identifying as LGBT, a rite-of-passage followed by immediate involvement in a proactive and healthy queer community, we help new and long-time members of our community, especially newly out queer youth, avoid unhealthy behaviors and destructive thought patterns.

They enter into a real community, in which all the members care about each other's well-being and try to help each other be as happy and healthy as possible, not a false community that just drinks at the same watering holes, reads the same papers and magazines, or joins the same organizations.

Whether anybody actually chooses to call themselves "Sidhe" doesn't matter; the term could just as easily be "Nommo" (after the wise, amphibious beings of the African Dogon tribe's legends) or anything else, or nothing at all, depending on the person. What matters is that we, as individuals and as queer communities, dedicate ourselves to establishing the Beloved Community using the Shirt of Flame. *Sidhe* is a convenient term for LGBT people who have made this kind of commitment—it's certainly a lot better than "Shirt of Flamers!"

As Sidhe, we take the first step toward the Beloved Community by beginning to build it in miniature; we start where we are, in our own towns, cities and neighborhoods. Our intentional Sidhe communities are not isolationist; they're right wherever we are. It wouldn't necessarily be helpful to build our own commune off in the queer wilds. We want to create change and develop our genuine Power by engaging the world, not escaping it. We do our most creative work in the midst of life, not far removed from it.

Instead, small groups of 4-12 Sidhe commit to the creative work of community-building, developing our genuine Power and ability to Love, perfecting the skills of "taking whole" in order to help others and ourselves achieve happiness and avoid suffering. Interacting with the same diverse group of LGBT people over time in a space that is safe for deep sharing, intimacy and exploration of Power, Love and Right Action, prepares us for the great work of building the larger Beloved Community, and sustains us through the sweat and tedium that will pave our way to victory.

These groups, or "circles," also help each individual participant achieve her or his personal happiness by creating what Julia Mossbridge, in her book, *Unfolding: The Perpetual Science of Your Soul's Work*, calls "Resonant, Growth and Goal Community." Sidhe circles are Resonant because the safe space created by a rule of nonjudgment allows each person to free themselves from self-imposed limitations and fears. By leaping (or crawling) over those boundaries, each person is able to resonate with the fullness of their beauty, power and freedom like a bell being struck, and the whole group supports their expression of who they are. The group provides feelings of groundedness, efficacy, value, social support, progression, self-knowledge and meaning. It's freeing that the other members of the group are open to witnessing your highest expression of Self, the too-secret-dream of you as you wish to be and fear becoming.

"When we reveal ourselves...and find that this brings healing rather than harm, we make an important discovery—that intimate relationship can provide a sanctuary from the world of facades, a sacred space where we can be ourselves, as we are...This kind of unmasking—speaking our truth, sharing our inner struggles, and revealing our raw edges—is sacred activity."

~ John Welwood

The circles are also Growth communities because everyone who participates in one opens herself to change. The diversity of the groups means that not everyone will be of the same opinion about everything.

There will be conflicts and challenges. However, because the nature of the group is to be supportive and focused on developing community despite differences, each Sidhe circle offers its members the chance to examine their feelings of conflict and search for the wisdom hidden in the anger or pain. Dealing with one's own assumptions and negativity alone can be overwhelming, but the Sidhe can "bring it to the circle" and receive the support and guidance of peers. Of course, in each group there will be "matches," people who find it easy to get along with each other, and "fits," those who have more difficulty being with each other, but who may have lessons to learn from each other.

That the circle members share common Goals is what enables circles to ultimately be helpful. Mossbridge calls a Goal community, "a group that strives toward a goal that is too large for any one individual in the group to meet." Every member of the group will bring unique insights and gifts to the work to accomplish the group's goals, and the group will remain flexible enough for every member to apply her or his gifts and insights. Although establishing the Beloved Community is the goal at the heart of every Sidhe circle, no one group can do it. Each group must choose its own areas to work in toward that goal.

These circles may form naturally—from a group of like-minded LGBT people who already know each other—or can be a random group of LGBT people thrown together by fate and their local LGBT community center after reading *Shirt of Flame*. However the members are chosen, each group should be cemented in some kind of ceremony, perhaps like the one described at the beginning of this chapter.

This ceremony can be both individual initiation into the Sidhe and the genesis of every Sidhe circle. It allows each Gay, Bi-affectionate, Transgender or Lesbian person to stand up in front of the larger queer and Ally community and proclaim the life they truly want. The ritual allows each of them to make a public commitment to using her or his unique insights and gifts to contribute to building the Beloved Community. Each group goes through the initiation together, and their mutual rite of passage honors and bonds the Resonant/Growth/Goal Community of their Sidhe circle, and prepares each member for the triumphant work of "arranging the ground" for the LGBT movement's ultimate victory.

4
FIRE IN THE LAKE

"The mind is not a vessel to be filled, but a fire to be ignited."

~ Plutarch

FOUR QUESTIONS

Now that we've established the moral principles of a Shirt of Flame movement and committed to creating change with other, like-minded same-gender-loving and transgender people through *Sidhe* circles, we still face the monumental task of enumerating precisely what kinds of resistance can emerge from these principles. Because our credibility is only maintained as long as our conduct unconditionally adheres to the moral principles we've outlined, the forms of our activism must always meet several criteria:

1. **Our activism must take no form that debilitates our potential for Power.**
   So all forms of physical, verbal and psychological attack, and all manipulative and disingenuous actions, must be dismissed.

2. **No just laws may be broken during the conduct of our resistance.**
   Maintaining our commitment to Law as the future guarantor of our rights and liberties is an important component of the trust we seek to build with society. If we disrespect Law, we disrespect society.

3. **Every act of resistance must be focused on *"taking whole."***
   The pure intention behind our every act of resistance must be to help self or others achieve happiness or avoid suffering, with the secondary knowledge that such actions develop communion and increase our genuine Power. Such activity will be called *Collective Cultivation.*

4. One's activism must be personally motivated, not engineered by others.

An individual's Shirt of Flame activism must arise naturally from a deeply personal desire to help self and others achieve happiness and avoid suffering. The individual activist takes action based on knowledge of their own purity of intention and what they are passionate about. The individual activist's resistance can be inspired or suggested by, but not dictated by, their Sidhe circle or movement leaders.

So, based on those criteria, when considering an action, we must first ask ourselves these Four Questions:

1. **Is it *Ahimsa* (non-harming)?**
2. **Is it congruous?**
3. **Is it Collective Cultivation?**
4. **Is it personal?**

Although Shirt of Flame activism is necessarily very personal, one's activism must not take place in a vacuum! Remember that it's an absolute imperative that one establish a *Sidhe* ("shee") circle of at least two partners, whenever possible, so that even a single LGBT individual's Shirt of Flame activism takes place in *community*. Participation in a circle of LGBT friends committed to Shirt of Flame principles enables the members of the group to work together to deepen their individual understanding and embodiment of the principles. Also, as we've discussed, Sidhe circles are also open, emotionally safe forums in which people can share their personal stories and growth as well as receive feedback from the group about the forms of their activism and decide on Collective Cultivation that members of the Sidhe circle can undertake together to help manifest the most compassionate society.

Like Rosa Parks refusing to move to the back of the bus, popularly considered the beginning of the African-American civil rights movement, a single person acting in isolation can be an effective activist. Even Ms. Parks, however, was part of a *community* of civil rights activists. In fact, she had been participating in resistance for over a decade! She'd spent *twelve years* helping lead her local NAACP chapter! Her courageous and celebrated act was the result of *years* of soulful preparation, education, experimentation and regular inspiration by her fellow activists. In *Soul of a Citizen: Living with Conviction in a Cynical Time*, Paul Rogat Loeb urges us to think about how Rosa Parks' historic action actually happened: "In the prevailing myth, Parks—a holy innocent—acts almost on a whim, in isolation. The lesson seems to be that if any of us suddenly got the urge to do something heroic, that would be great. Of course most of us wait our entire lives for the ideal moment.

"The real story is more empowering: It suggests that change is the product of deliberate, incremental action. When we join together to shape a better world, sometimes our struggles will fail or bear only modest fruits. Other times they will trigger miraculous outpourings of courage and heart. We can never know beforehand what the consequences of our actions will be."

"Do not depend on the hope of results. You may have to face the fact that your work will be apparently worthless and even achieve no result at all, if not perhaps results opposite to what you expect. As you get used to this idea, you start more and more to concentrate not on the results, but on the value, the rightness, the truth of the work itself. You gradually struggle less and less for an idea and more and more for specific people. In the end, it is the reality of personal relationship that saves everything."

~ Thomas Merton

"Deliberate, incremental action" is the substance of "taking whole," and it's vital that LGBT individuals support each other in taking the small steps that make up our journey to the Beloved Community. We also need to reorganize the LGBT community as a whole to do everything possible to make that journey possible.

Sidhe circles take the role that the NAACP took in Rosa Park's life by offering their members constant guidance, practice, inspiration and empowerment. The circles also act as a check on ill-considered or incongruous activism, since the members discuss actions with the group before undertaking them. The members of the circle remind one another of what the real goals of the LGBT Movement are, help each other consider the Four Questions, and gently allow everyone to express and transcend their natural afflictive emotions about oppression and violence without acting out in negative, destructive ways. The circles will also prove to be an important font of new forms of queer activism—held to the Four Questions—that transcend traditional forms of nonviolent resistance.

OPPROBRIUM

A cursory look at traditional nonviolent resistance reveals two basic forms: Noncooperation and Direct Action. Acts of Noncooperation are individuals refusing to support or participate in what they see as wrong. For example, this could mean refusing to pay the portion of your income tax that supports excessive military spending, refusing to register for the draft, union strikes or sweatshop boycotts. Direct Actions include anything that addresses the actual cause of your concern— whether that's fighting hunger by feeding someone or protecting an old-growth forest by living in a redwood tree. For our purposes, Direct Actions also include symbolic protest actions, for example, civil disobedience. Symbolic protest actions are public protests that seek to call attention to an issue, such as pouring blood onto missiles, or that break unjust laws—like Black folks sitting at "Whites Only" lunch counters during the African-American civil rights movement.

Direct Actions often involve the willingness of the activist to suffer during or because of the Direct Action (i.e. to perhaps be spat on, slandered, beaten, arrested, fired, etc.). This suffering is called *voluntary redemptive suffering*: "voluntary" because each activist that participates in the direct action has consciously decided that breaking the unjust law is more important than her or his safety, and that she or he will not flee from the repercussions nor retaliate; and "redemptive" because the activist hopes that his or her suffering will liberate the oppressors and lead to freedom and justice for both oppressed and oppressor.

Voluntary redemptive suffering was justifiable during the Indian Independence movement and the African-American civil rights movement because the violation of unjust laws with the goal of reform and redemption was a central purpose of those movements. Moreover, those oppressed people had no other outlet to express outrage or effect change—they could not, for example, organize to vote their oppressors out of office.

The unjust laws and policies that discriminate against LGBT people do not lend themselves to similar voluntary redemptive suffering. Today's nonviolent gay activists who choose voluntary redemptive suffering (usually arrest) do so as an entirely symbolic action—the laws they break are trespassing or unlawful-assembly statutes and not *unjust* laws or policies which directly discriminate against LGBT people. Instead of breaking unjust laws in the name of justice like Gandhi and King, their voluntary redemptive suffering has three goals:

1. To demonstrate the protesters' commitment to non-retaliation even when directly confronted by suffering, hatred and violence;

2. To induce pity in those who witness it. Pity, you remember, is the near enemy of compassion;

3. And finally, their voluntary redemptive suffering is intended to promote *opprobrium* in their oppressors— "the shame and disgrace attached to improper conduct." Ideally, this afflictive emotion is so intense that the oppressor realizes that his or her actions, opinions, or laws must be unjust because he or she feels so badly about the activists' suffering as a direct result of those actions/opinions/laws.

These activists sincerely believe that the opprobrium their voluntary redemptive suffering engenders is a natural and appropriate afflictive emotion for their oppressors to feel. They believe that by inducing negatives (suffering, shame and disgrace, and pity) they are able to achieve their desired end: an awakening of new moral awareness in some of the oppressors that amends their unjust beliefs and behavior. This approach ignores the basic tenet upon which all nonviolence is based: *the end is inherent in the means.* The science of social alchemy is not magnetic—a negative does not attract a positive.

While voices should be raised to 'speak truth to power' in protest against injustice, the effort to make change must not pass the boundary into intentionally causing suffering. The first Question, *"Is it Ahimsa?"* must be carefully considered regarding modern voluntary redemptive suffering and its unique method of violence—that it intentionally causes the activists to suffer and induces opprobrium and/or pity in others. Indeed, imitating the traditional technique of voluntary redemptive suffering only adds to the level of pain and violence in the world instead of relieving suffering and reducing violence. To approach creating a society based on cultivation, we must pursue a purer nonviolence. To pursue a purer nonviolence, we must use the "deliberate and incremental" means of Collective Cultivation available to us that cause no suffering of any kind intentionally, however justifiable the end.

The science of social alchemy is not magnetic—
a negative does not attract a positive.

LGBT activists cannot participate in proper civil disobedience by mimicking the techniques that worked for Gandhi and King, that is, by readily and *en masse* risking voluntary redemptive suffering by breaking laws that do not discriminate against us, because the truest civil disobedience breaks *unjust* laws in the name of justice. There's an inherent contradiction in breaking *just* laws in the name of justice. To do so shows fundamental disrespect for Law as the means by which our republic functions and damages public perception of our commitment to Justice. If we cannot tell good laws from bad, how can we be trusted to suggest good ones? *Pursuing voluntary redemptive suffering is incongruous with our ultimate goals, and does not increase our genuine Power.* With so much suffering, opprobrium and pity, there are just too many negatives involved to ultimately create a positive. If "the end is inherent in the means," then this is not the pure nonviolence to which we must aspire in order to manifest a purely nonviolent society. We have better options.

THE CAUSES OF THE SAINTS

> "At the center of the universe is a loving heart that continues to beat and that wants the best for every person. Anything we can do to help foster the intellect and spirit and emotional growth of our fellow human beings, that is our job. Those of us who have this particular vision must continue against all odds. Life is for service."
>
> ~ Fred Rogers of "Mister Rogers"

Founded by Rev. Dr. Mel White and his partner, Gary Nixon, Soulforce, Inc., is an interfaith organization that uses nonviolent techniques to fight homophobia and discrimination in faith communities. In their own words, Soulforce is dedicated to "ending spiritual violence perpetuated by religious policies and teachings against GLBT people." Soulforce is also one of the few organizations leading the way in the direction of pure nonviolence.

In October 2000, Soulforce joined with Habitat for Humanity to construct a home for a disadvantaged family in Lynchburg, Virginia, home of the infamous Reverend Jerry Falwell and his Liberty University and Thomas Road Baptist Church. LGBT and Ally "Soulforcees" joined together in the most public example of Shirt of Flame nonviolence of the new century; theirs was the first Direct Action to affirmatively answer all of the Four Questions. Their construction of a home for the Hintons was *Ahimsa*, congruous with every goal of the Movement, and a very personal example of collective cultivation. In fact, if members of Falwell's Thomas Road Baptist Church had helped construct the home as promised, the project would also have been an important example of building communion with 'the enemy.'

This wonderful example of pure nonviolence illustrates perhaps the most valuable path to being 21st Century *Satyagrahi*, the essence of being one of the Sidhe, the crux of wearing the Shirt of Flame: *Voluntary Redemptive Service*. This kind of compassionate, purely nonviolent action on behalf of self and others offers the remittance of our perceived deviance and moral inadequacies, develops our genuine Power, and demonstrates our individual and collective commitment to proactively create a better world for everyone. Such Voluntary Redemptive Service, honestly undertaken to relieve suffering and approach self- and social-actualization, is one of the best techniques our Shirt of Flame activism has to eliminate the basis of all discrimination against us Bisexual, Gay, Transgender and Lesbian people—erroneous, negative attitudes about our propriety and our value. All of us can encourage change, reform and evolution in others and organizations through our cultivating *example.*

Imagine if each Transgender, Lesbian, Bisexual and Gay person dedicated a portion of her or his time to help others achieve happiness and avoid or reduce suffering: LGBT people directly serving the poor, the sick, the hungry, the homeless, the disenfranchised, the elderly, or the disaster-stricken with complete, conscientious and non-aggressive honesty—as each LGBT person feels called to do so by her or his personal passions. All of us have gifts to offer those in real, immediate need, even if only the gift of a hand to hold or our simple presence. If we considered it, each of us could think of some situation or life in which we could make a difference, and in which we would like to make a difference.

Imagine groups of us going out every Saturday afternoon into the shadowy corners of cities and doing what needs to be done.

Imagine the 'barn-raisings' that could be accomplished every weekend if we all helped. Imagine the sustainably designed cottages we could build to temporarily house and employ the homeless.

Imagine coalitions of us gathering world class architects, arcologists, and businesses to work with residents to revitalize inner cities!

Imagine building coalitions to buy endangered forests and wetlands.

Imagine planting vegetable gardens on roofs and parking lots.

Imagine tutoring, mentoring, crisis counseling, mowing lawns, fetching groceries, painting houses and murals.

Imagine the feeling of holding the children, the despairing, the dying.

Imagine the transformative power such experiences would have on our own lives and on every life we touched in the process.

Do you think negative attitudes about our propriety and our value could persist if we were living the evidence to the contrary all around our detractors? if we were solving the societal problems that divide the interests of people of conscience and propagate destructive thought patterns? Of course not! *Over time, by claiming full participation in our com-*

munities through relentless, proactive and purely nonviolent collective cultivation, we will win our case in the hearts and minds of our oppressors.

"In the pioneering days individualism could survive because the objective was to build a homestead and acquire personal property. Now we are faced with the task of building a community and a society, which means interdependence, interconnectedness and integration. Exclusivity must give way to inclusivity if living in peace and harmony are our objectives. The choice before humanity in the next millennium, therefore, is: Learn to respect life or live to regret it."

~ Arun Gandhi

Our Voluntary Redemptive Service is ultimately a function of our desire to deeply understand Interdependence, and how we can achieve happiness and avoid suffering in an interdependent world. We must be careful to not approach Voluntary Redemptive Service from the idea that we have arrived to 'raise up the oppressed and disadvantaged'. This only creates an egotistical hierarchy, with us at the top and 'those poor unfortunates' at the bottom. Again, compassion is helpful; pity is not. We can only build communion with those we serve by interacting with them as equal partners in the communal body and not as some kind of separate class. We are aware that we may have more material wealth, education or expertise than some others, but, in the end, the goal is to perceive others through interdependent eyes. Developing this horizontal perception will enable us to excel in the coming era of Interdependence—we will have the interdependent skills and community to survive and flourish, while those who persist in attacking, dividing and judging will have (and cause) difficulty. It would be helpful for each LGBT person to engage in a process of self-examination of her or his own internalized homophobia or genderphobia, racism, sexism, and classism before venturing too far into the community. Resources for such 'cleansing' are available on www.fireinthelake.com.

Voluntary Redemptive Service must be a personal commitment to volunteer to help a community, organization, individual or family that has nothing directly to do with "gay rights" whatsoever. We all have other issues we care about, and joining with others to redress those issues (by cultivating well-being or reducing suffering) is the essence of

Sidhe activism.

Ideally, one's personal commitment to help should be sustained over a period of time. We may have a tendency to sweep in, fix something or alleviate a condition, and then sweep right back out again. Such dilettantism is not *un*helpful, but also does not fully develop communion. After Soulforce built the Habitat for Humanity house in Lynchburg, Mel White and his partner actually *moved* there, right across the street from Falwell's church! They're active in the community and even attend Falwell's church! Their focus remains on LGBT affirmation, but they are also developing long-term personal relationships that may stimulate real change.

Let's consider a hypothetical example to see how a sustained commitment to a Voluntary Redemptive Service project might be helpful. Say the members of a Sidhe circle decide to renovate an inner city health clinic over a long weekend. All by themselves, they repaint the interior, cover the graffiti outside, fix the leaky faucet in the bathroom, repair the front steps, add a wheelchair ramp and mount a new sign—then, come Monday, return to their lives feeling pretty good about themselves and never visit the clinic again. Obviously, the service they accomplished is quite wonderful, and probably very helpful and welcome to the clinic. Surely when they returned to the clinic on Monday, the clinicians would appreciate those kind gay folks' labor!

The labor, however, is not the only point. Touching the lives of *people*—and therefore building both enriching relationships and our genuine Power—is the more important goal. Voluntary Redemptive Service can answer all Four Questions affirmatively, but still will not be completely effective if it does not answer the fourth Question twice. As we have already discussed, "Is it personal?" requires that the service be a personally motivated act of each one of the Sidhe. At the same time, Voluntary Redemptive Service, and Shirt of Flame activism in general, suggests that the service, the activism, must also be *inter*-personal. To return to our example, the service would have been more completely effective if:

> a) The renovation of the clinic had included the clinicians and those the clinic serves, so that everyone was working together for the common good; and,

b) If the Sidhe circle had developed long-term
relationships based on personal involvement with the
clinicians and those served—returning frequently to
that clinic and community and getting to know those
people.

The desire to meet and know our fellow human beings— to find out
how they live, to understand our interdependent relationship and to
help all of us achieve happiness and avoid suffering—is the interpersonal
root of Voluntary Redemptive Service. Without consistent commitment, Voluntary Redemptive Service only suggests an assumption of
debt—"we helped you out, now you thank us for it by helping us out
in the voting booth come November," or an equivalent. Even an unar-
ticulated obligation is detrimental to deep communion and genuine
Power. As Miguel de Cervantes wrote in *Don Quixote*, "The obligations
that spring from benefits and kindnesses received are ties that prevent
a noble mind from ranging freely. Happy the man to whom Heaven has
given a morsel of bread for which he is obliged to thank Heaven alone."
This is why we relinquish our 'LGBT self-interest'—we do not only do
this work in order to make people appreciate LGBT folks, or to get
them to vote a certain way, or even to change their hearts and minds.
Make no mistake, those are desirable *by-products* of Voluntary
Redemptive Service! They cannot, however, be the *goals* of the work,
or Voluntary Redemptive Service becomes merely a manipulative agent
of old-school power, and loses the name of pure nonviolence.

Collective Cultivation's motivation must be each LGBT person's simple, heartfelt vision of what a better world would look like, and their
dedication to that vision. Collective Cultivation—our new kind of
Direct Action, of which Voluntary Redemptive Service is the main technique—is the proactive commitment of each Shirt of Flame activist to
help manifest his or her personal vision of a Beloved Community. A pri-
mary goal of these actions is to carry those visions into reality, while
maintaining at all times his or her spirit and practice of pure nonviolence of heart, tongue and fist. Of course, a prerequisite for Voluntary
Redemptive Service is that the individual serve as an openly (although
not confrontationally) LGBT person—complete, conscientious and non-
aggressive honesty about one's sexual orientation and/or gender identi-

ty while undertaking service is part of the directness of one's action.

Unfortunately, voluntary redemptive suffering may occur in the process of Voluntary Redemptive Service, but, in this case, would be without any element of intentional suffering, opprobrium or pity. We may be welcomed with violence when we offer Voluntary Redemptive Service, or find violence upon us suddenly like a pit bull in a cathedral, but at least our intention will be pure. There's always the possibility that we may suffer for our activism, but without inviting or causing our's or others' suffering.

LGBT people's Collective Cultivation will create positive change in the circumstances of our fellow human beings and communities. We will let "justice roll down like waters, and righteousness like an ever-flowing stream" into the parched wasteland. The weight of our good will and compassionate deeds will build the foundation for the ultimate reversal of queer people's fortune and status in society.

"The best lack all conviction, while the worst / Are full of passion-ate intensity," W.B. Yeats wrote in "The Second Coming," and that is frequently our experience in society. That sorry state of affairs is a choice, and we can choose again. We can wear our Shirts of Flame and go fiery and fearless into the darkness, plunge our still-burning arms into inky waters to save the embryonic Beloved Community from drowning. We Lesbian, Gay, Bisexual and Transgender women and men can recreate our lives, our relationships, our activism and our role in society. That is how the *Satyagrahi* become the *Sidhe*. That is how we become the change we wish to see in the world. That is how we final-ly become free.

AFTERWORD
TEMPLEISEN

You now know that genuine Power results from communion, which in turn is rooted in compassion and Love, and that any form of violence, whether of fist, tongue or heart, destroys your potential for Power in an interdependent world. When you have declared your commitment to using the Shirt of Flame to create change, you become a healing, creative force in the world and in other people's lives—a kind of human Holy Grail.

Familiar to most of us from childhood stories of King Arthur, the symbolism of the legendary Grail has two very different origins: the pre-Christian Western European legend of a supernatural supply of bountiful goodness—the "horn of plenty"—and the early Christian tale of the "Cup of Christ" from the Last Supper, which legend tells us Joseph of Arimathea used to catch the blood of Jesus on the cross and subsequently brought with him to the island of Britain. Each of these two legends informs the meaning of the Grail as a universally relevant symbol: a sacred source from which flows limitless life, abundance and healing.

In the chivalrous Arthurian romance of the knight Perceval and his search for the Holy Grail, Perceval's quest leads him into the realm of an unknown King. The King and his kingdom are sick and dying. The realm is becoming literally and metaphorically a wasteland, the green dying and the people living hollow, inauthentic and desperate lives. Perceval sees a procession of weeping courtiers bearing the ailing King and preceded by the floating Grail. His instinct is to ask what is wrong and how he can help, but because of his knightly instruction to avoid idle and uninvited chatter, he does not. Because he acts out of what he was taught and not what he feels—he does not follow his inner guide, his "Grail-nature" as it were—the procession disappears and Perceval leaves without asking his question and both land and King remain ill. The adventure fails.

After five years of wandering, Perceval finds his way back to the castle where he saw the Grail. This time, he asks his question, "What ails the king?" and miraculously, the Grail pours forth its healing power on the King and on the land. To manifest its power, the Grail requires the willingness of the individual to open her or his human heart to another. To work, the Grail—as symbol of the inexhaustible source of life— requires a spontaneous compassion, a communion, a Love.

LGBT people who use the Shirt of Flame choose to open their hearts like Perceval to the Grail King, and like the Grail upon his kingdom. Your inner work is to discover or create ports of entry within yourself to the Grail-like font of life, joy and harmony-affirming energy and knowledge that lies within you. When you claim a "Grail-nature" by donning the Shirt of Flame and joining the Sidhe, you become like a chalice containing the bubbling spring of Love-as-action from which all healing proceeds. Once emptied of all that is not Love-affirming, you become a channel through which new connectivity and transformation can pour into this world of ignorance, politics, compromise and violence. There is only Power in such joining and becoming, in motion, in conscious evolution. In acquiescence, in self-absorption, in silence, there are only drawn-out endings.

This, then, is your quest, your mission: commit yourself to Love and use Collective Cultivation to co-create a social space of peace, harmony and well-being. Combined with the efforts of other Lesbian, Gay, Bisexual and Transgender people, you will help build a chorus of firm and gentle "No's" to all that threatens our human potential for greatness, a chorus that will deafen the entrenched powers and return hearing (seeing, breathing, motion) to the quiescent masses. The resounding "Yes!" that you offer so relentlessly through your Sidhe activism will echo through history as pivotal to the ultimate establishment of the Beloved Community, and the lives touched by your Voluntary Redemptive Service will create a ripple effect of opening hearts and minds across families, neighborhoods, cities and cultures. You are the one the world has been waiting for. Don't make us wait any longer!

WHAT NOW?

Visit www.fireinthelake.com to discuss your thoughts after reading
Shirt of Flame: The Secret Gay Art of War!

Interact with other readers, start a Sidhe circle,
read Ko's FIRE IN THE LAKE columns,
register for free stuff,
or tell your story of Collective Cultivation at:

www.fireinthelake.com

RECOMMENDED READING AND SOURCE MATERIAL

Order your favorites today through www.fireinthelake.com!

Joseph Campbell. *Hero with a Thousand Faces*. Princeton University Press, 1973. ISBN 0-691-01784-0. The myth of Prince Five-Weapons is recounted in Campbell's book.
————. *The Power of Myth*. Doubleday, 1988. ISBN 0-385-41886-8.

Margaret Wheatley. "Consumed by Either Fire or Fire: Journeying with T.S. Eliot," *Journal of Noetic Science*, November 1999. www.margaretwheatley.com.
————. *Turning to One Another: Simple Conversations to Restore Hope to the Future*. Berrett-Koehler, 2002. ISBN 1576751457.

T.S. Eliot. *Four Quartets*. Harvest Books, 1974. ISBN 0156332256. "Shirt of Flame" is taken from the poem, "Little Gidding".

Marianne Williamson. *Enchanted Love: The Mystical Power of Intimate Relationships*. Touchstone Books, 2001. ISBN 0684870258.
————. *Healing the Soul of America: Reclaiming Our Voices as Spiritual Citizens*. Touchstone Books, 2000. ISBN 0684846225. Read this book for an excellent analysis of Democratic First Principles.
————. *Illuminata: Thoughts, Prayers, Rites of Passage*. Random House, 1994. ISBN 0679435506.

H.H. The 14th Dalai Lama. *Ethics for the New Millennium*. Riverhead Books, 1999. ISBN 1-57322-025-6. The ideas for the Universal Ethical Standard are from His Holiness' book.

Sir Richard Rogers. *Cities for a Small Planet*. Westview Press, 1997. ISBN 0-8133-3553-1. My broad definition of a Beloved Community is taken from Rogers'description of a sustainable city.

Paul Ray and Sherry Ruth Anderson. *The Cultural Creatives: How 50 Million People are Changing the World*. Three Rivers Press, 2001. ISBN 0609808451.

Ken Wilber. *A Brief History of Everything*. Shambhala Publications, Inc., 1996. ISBN 1-57062-187-X.

————. *A Theory of Everything: An Integral Vision for Business, Politics, Science and Spirituality*. Shambhala Publications, Inc., 2000. ISBN 1-57062-855-6.

————. *One Taste: Daily Reflections on Integral Spirituality*. Random House, 2000. ISBN 1570625476.

Paulo Freire. *Pedagogy of the Oppressed*. Continuum International Publishing Group, 2000. ISBN 0-8264-1276-9.

Dean Ornish. *Love and Survival: The Scientific Basis for the Healing Power of Intimacy*. HarperCollins, 1999. ISBN 0060930209.

————. "Health", essay from *Imagine: What America Could be in the 21st Century*. Rodale, Inc., 2000. ISBN 1-57954-302-2. This is an important collection of essays suggesting healthy ways for the USA to move toward the Beloved Community. Purchases benefit Global Renaissance Alliance.

Robert Greene. *The 48 Laws of Power*. Penguin USA, 2000. ISBN 0140280197. Interested in the history of traditional power? Read this book.

Mark Thompson. *Gay Soul: Finding the Heart of Gay Spirit and Nature with Sixteen Writers, Healers, Teachers, and Visionaries*. Harper San Francisco, 1995. ISBN 006251041X.

Tara Bennett-Goleman. *Emotional Alchemy: How the Mind can Heal the Heart*. Three Rivers Press, 2002. ISBN 0609809032.

Andrew Cohen. *Living Enlightenment: A Call for Evolution Beyond Ego*. Moksha Press, 2002. ISBN 188392930X.

Alvin Toffler. *Future Shock*. Bantam Books, 1991. ISBN 0553277375.

YES! A Journal of Positive Futures. www.yesmagazine.org. The explanation of power the Navajo medicine man told to Carolyn Raffensperger is from YES! Magazine's Winter 2001 issue (#16).

bell hooks. *All About Love: New Visions*. HarperCollins, 2000. ISBN 0-688-16844-2
————. "Everlasting Love" Lecture given at Renaissance Unity in Warren, Michigan, February 9, 2001.

M. Scott Peck. *The Road Less Traveled, 25th Anniversary Edition: A New Psychology of Love, Traditional Values and Spiritual Growth*. Touchstone Books, 2003. ISBN 0743243153.

Bjork. "All is Full of Love" from the album, *Homogenic*. Elektra, 1997. ASIN B000002HPV.

Mohandas K. Gandhi. Sir Richard Attenborough, Ed. *The Words of Gandhi*. Newmarket Press, 1996. ISBN 0-55704-290-X.

Nathaniel Brandon. *The Six Pillars of Self-Esteem*. Bantam Books, 1995. ISBN 0553374397.

David G. Myers, PH.D. *The Pursuit of Happiness: Discovering the Pathway to Fulfillment, Well-Being, and Enduring Personal Joy*. Avon Books, 1992. ISBn 0-380-71522-8. Dave is an incredible human being and an accomplished and respected Ally. He not only taught Ko's Psychology course, he also attended Ko and Mike's wedding! This book is highly recommended for everyone who wants to delve deeper into their own happiness.

Ayya Khema. *Visible Here and Now: The Buddha's Teachings on the Rewards of Spiritual Practice*. Shambhala Publications, 2001. ISBN 1570624925.

Roshi Bernie Glassman. *Bearing Witness: A Zen Master's Lessons in Making Peace*. Random House, 1999. ISBN 0609803913.

Fritjof Capra. *The Tao of Physics: An Exploration of the Parallels Between Modern Physics and Eastern Mysticism*. Shambhala Publications, 2000. ISBN 1570625190.

Thich Nhat Hanh. *Being Peace*. Parallax Press, 1988. ISBN 0938077007.

Sun Tzu. Translation, Essays and Commentary by the Denma Translation Group. *The Art of War: A New Translation*. Shambhala Publications, 2001. ISBN 1-57062-552-2. www.victoryoverwar.com.

The Denma Translation Group. "The Sage Commander" from Shambhala Sun Magazine, January 2001. www.shambhalasun.com.

Martin Luther King, Jr. *A Testament of Hope: Essential Writings and Speeches of Martin Luther King, Jr.* Harper San Francisco, 1991. ISBN 0060646918.

Julia Mossbridge. *Unfolding: The Perpetual Science of Your Soul's Work*. New World Library, 2002. ISBN 1-57731-193-0.

Paul Rogat Loeb. *Soul of a Citizen: Living With Conviction in a Cynical Time*. St. Martin's Press, 1999. ISBN 0312204353.

George Leonard and Michael Murphy. *The Life We are Given: A Long-Term Program for Realizing the Potential of Body, Mind, Heart, and Soul*. Tarcher/Putnam, 1995. ISBN 0-87477-792-5.

Toby Johnson. *Gay Perspective: Things Our Homosexuality Tells Us About the Nature of God and the Universe*. Alyson Publications, 2003. ISBN 155583762X.

ABOUT THE AUTHOR

Ko Imani is a widely-read writer, social entrepreneur and agent of change.

Ko's FIRE IN THE LAKE columns are already revolutionizing the way Lesbian, Gay, Bisexual and Transgender people approach their personal relationships and their activism. Ko gives away his monthly FIRE IN THE LAKE columns to LGBT nonprofits—including community centers, faith communities, 'zines and PFLAG chapters—for their newsletters and websites, through which Ko is touching the lives of almost one million LGBT and Ally people.

"I think that if everyone shares *Shirt of Flame: The Secret Gay Art of War* with their LGBT friends and family, this book will be the catalyst for a real revolution, not only as far as teaching LGBT people the secrets of their ultimate liberation, but also permanently changing society for the better," says Ko. "We all know that the human race can't go on with all this fear and violence. It's time to make a change, and I believe that LGBT people have an important role to play. Only *Shirt of Flame* explains what that role is and how we can claim it."

Ko and his husband, Michael, were married in Grand Rapids, Michigan, on June 25, 2000, and currently live near Ann Arbor, Michigan.